To *the*
TENTH
GENERATION

God's Heart *for* Your Family,
Far Into the Future

To the
TENTH
GENERATION

RAY & JANI ORTLUND

B&H
PUBLISHING®
BRENTWOOD, TENNESSEE

Published by B&H Publishing Group
Brentwood, Tennessee

Dewey Decimal Classification: 306.85
Subject Heading: FAMILY LIFE \
GENERATIONS \ CHRISTIAN LIFE

Italics used in Scripture references are added
by the author to express emphasis.

Cover design and illustration by Ligia Teodosiu.

1 2 3 4 5 6 • 27 26 25 24.

To the memory of
Hope Anastasia Ortlund,
our grandchild happy in God's presence above
while we rejoice in him here below

Contents

Foreword

Let me begin by stating the obvious: no family is perfect. Considering this, what would compel a husband and wife to write a book on a potentially sensitive subject and run the risk of inviting scrutiny and suspicion into their own family? Quite simply: faith. This book attests to a faith-filled conviction that amid the potential pitfalls and inevitable shortcomings, building a family with a vision of expanding God's kingdom is a worthy endeavor packed with eternal potential and is actually possible for every one of us.

Because this book is in your hands, I suspect you have a desire to build a family that will echo with redemptive reverberations for generations to come. Read on. You have two trustworthy trail guides in the pages ahead. They are not saying, "Look at us and follow us because we did it perfectly." Rather, they are saying, "Look with us at this vision God has placed on our hearts. With his help you can build a family of generational devotion to Christ, as we are seeking to do."

Proverbs 29:18 can be translated, "Where there is no prophetic vision the people are discouraged." This book, with the prophetic vision it boldly casts, was written to *encourage* you. As an Ortlund insider (I am Ray and Jani's daughter), I can testify to the astonishing privilege of growing up in a home of such consistent love, nurture, wisdom, kindness, truth, and grace. It's equipped me well to carry the baton of disciple-making into my own mothering amid very challenging circumstances.

As you read this book, may your heart swell with hope and catch the vision of what your family can become in Christ, and may you be equipped and encouraged in your endeavor.

Krista Ortlund Scheidt

PART I

In Your Family

CHAPTER 1

Your Future Is Bigger than You Think

"All these blessings shall come upon
you and overtake you."
Deuteronomy 28:2

You are a person of historic significance. Maybe you don't see yourself that way. Maybe you feel small. Who doesn't? But if it's true, if it's true that you are *historically significant,* then your life is also *eternally consequential.* You live in a much bigger space and time than you think, bearing a much larger capacity for influence than you might realize.

Let's think it through together.

The world trivializes us. It wears us down day after day. The message coming through the cultural air we breathe is that we're nothing more than our social media following, nothing

3

more than a unit in a voting bloc, nothing more than a statistic in a marketing niche. And when this world is not trivializing us, it's mistreating us. It leaves us feeling not only small but also damaged, as if we needed any more help causing trouble to ourselves or thinking poorly of ourselves!

No surprise, then, that we sometimes wonder, *Why try at all? Why not just settle?*

But we do matter. *You* matter. You matter right now, this very instant as you read these words, and you will matter forever. Why? Because God himself created you for a purpose so big that only he could dream it up and pull it off.

Almighty God orchestrated your entrance into history. Throughout your preceding generations, he was preparing your very DNA for your mission here in his world. He arranged everything through human events for you to be born in the right place, at the right time, for the right reason. And every single day since then, he's been investing in you, through both your joys and your sorrows. You are the only one on the face of the earth who can fulfill God's mission for *you.*

Why not dare to believe it? You really are a person of historic significance. God thinks so. He has a plan in motion, a plan that he's great at working, and his plan includes you. In fact, he "works *all things* according to the counsel of his will" (Eph. 1:11). How can that *not* include you?

And if it includes you, doesn't it include your family too?

4

If your life is no accident of fate, then your marriage and children are no accident either—including that "surprise" baby you didn't budget for. (We have one of those!) God has a thrilling purpose for your family, a purpose that runs far past the immediate present, a purpose that extends long into the future.

That is why we wrote this book—to get you thinking bigger thoughts about yourself and your family's place in God's plan. Bigger thoughts grow bigger faith. And your faith will change the story your life will tell for generations to come.

Decades from now, long after you're at home with the Lord in eternal glory, your children will remember you. They will forget many things you say, but they will never forget who you were, who you *are*. They will never forget that you saw yourself (and them) the way God sees you and them, as people of historic significance, as part of his big plan for time and eternity. This whole miracle of his grace that you *are*, the glory of the Lord resting upon you even in your weakness—especially in your weakness—this is the "you" your children will never forget. In times of temptation they may *want* to forget. But they can never unsee what they are seeing in you—imperfect but Christlike, weak but powerful, ordinary but significant.

Many years from now, when they are in their fifties and sixties and seventies, facing challenges we cannot even imagine, they will gain courage just by remembering you. They will even turn aside at times to be alone and quietly weep with gratitude, thinking of your love for Jesus, your reverence for the Bible, your loyalty to your church, your steady faithfulness to earn and provide and give and pray, your sacrificial service to them through the years, your hope in God through thick and thin. They'll remember how you found significance in doing small things that didn't matter to this world, but they mattered to God, like you matter to him, like your family matters to him. By his grace, your children will then hand down that same gift to their children, and on into the future, until it becomes your family's generational story of what God can do through broken people who find their identity as children of the heavenly Father.

And you know what? They might keep telling that story *for a long time.*

Even to the tenth generation.

What Got Us Thinking

For us, long-term thinking about our family was a big change. Thinking out two weeks ahead, even two years ahead—we knew something about that. But thinking out, say, two hundred years? Those were completely unexplored thoughts!

Here is what opened our eyes. Years ago, Jani was reading her Bible . . .

———

. . . just enjoying my morning devotions—reading in Deuteronomy, no less—when something leapt off the page at me:

> "No one born of a forbidden union may enter the assembly of the LORD. *Even to the tenth generation,* none of his descendants may enter the assembly of the LORD. No Ammonite or Moabite may enter the assembly of the LORD. *Even to the tenth generation,* none of them may enter the assembly of the LORD forever." (Deut. 23:2–3)

Whoa, I thought. *That's serious! God excluding a group of people from entering his presence? For ten generations? How does that make sense?* If every page of the Bible, from cover to cover, is ultimately meant to show us Jesus and his gospel—every story, every law, every prophecy, every bit of it—what part of the good news was I supposed to see in something like this?

Well, we know the book of Deuteronomy is Moses preparing Israel for their future in the Promised Land, having come out of Egypt and traveled forty years through the wilderness. Part of that future included gathering for worship. And if we learn anything about worship from the way it's presented to us in these early pages of Scripture, it's that no one can ever just barge into God's presence, right? Everyone needs a sacrifice. Everyone needs the grace of Christ for sinners. Whatever else is going on in this Old Testament passage, it must be preparing us somehow for the assurance of the New Testament, that in Jesus alone, we who do not deserve to stand before a holy God—any more than these ancient sinners from Deuteronomy 23—have been invited and welcomed into his presence (see Acts 11:17–18; Gal. 2:15–16).

Oh, my, the thoughts were really swirling in my mind now. I was asking the Lord for help to see his heart more clearly. That's when a new thought occurred to me: "If God *excluded* certain people to the tenth generation, how much more does he long to *include* people to the tenth generation!" Doesn't he always delight more to bless than curse, to receive than reject, to welcome than banish? Yes. Much, much more!

> "If God *excluded* certain people to the tenth generation, how much more does he long to *include* people to the tenth generation!"

I shared this insight with Ray, and we began noticing that this deeply felt eagerness of God to smile upon his people with blessing is all over the Bible:

- "I will *bless* you." (Gen. 12:2)
- "Say to them, 'The LORD *bless* you and keep you.'" (Num. 6:23–24)
- "The LORD your God turned the curse into a *blessing* for you, because the LORD your God loved you." (Deut. 23:5)
- "All these *blessings* shall come upon you and overtake you." (Deut. 28:2)
- "I have set before you life and death, *blessing* and curse. Therefore choose life, that you and your offspring may live." (Deut. 30:19)
- Our God turned the curse into a *blessing*. (Neh. 13:2)
- Let them curse, but you will *bless*! (Ps. 109:28)
- A faithful man will abound with *blessings*. (Prov. 28:20)
- . . . so that in Christ Jesus the *blessing* of Abraham might come to the Gentiles, so that we might receive the promised Spirit through faith. (Gal. 3:14)
- Blessed be the God and Father of our Lord Jesus Christ, who has *blessed* us in Christ with every spiritual *blessing* in the heavenly places. (Eph. 1:3)

The bias of God's heart tilts *way* over toward including us in his blessing. That's the wraparound message we want to declare throughout this book. If, back in Deuteronomy, God banned certain tribes and groups "to the tenth generation," *how might the how-much-more heart of God bless our family, and your family, to the tenth generation?*

———

It's a thought that has really enlarged our categories. The generational blessing of God, stretching out over our family far into the distant future, left us breathless—more excited, and more responsible.

More excited? Yes! We started thinking about our family in expanded dimensions, beyond just the children and grand-children we know and love right now. *More responsible?* Yes! We began daring to pray more boldly, asking the Lord to bless our family, not vaguely, in general, but to the tenth generation. And if a generation comes of age every twenty years or so, we're now praying that every one of our descendants would love the Lord Jesus Christ with a true heart, above all else, for the next *two hundred years!*

Sometimes this vision for our family feels crazy even to us. But then we remember, God himself has been preparing us for this mission our whole lives. We are preapproved by his grace to "go for it"—in prayer, in purpose. We therefore accept responsibility to be flow-through-able as parents and grand-parents, inspiring our future generations to stand for Christ, far into the future..

And when you think about it, ten generations are not an unimaginably long time. The two of us already have a living experience of *five* generations within our own family: 1) our grandparents, 2) our parents, 3) ourselves, 4) our children, 5) our grandchildren. The story is big, yes. But look how quickly it unfolds.

The more we talked about it, the more thrillingly mind-boggling it became.

Here's what we mean. We got married in 1971. Just the two of us, obviously. And we weren't even thinking beyond our wedding night! The only thing we knew was that we couldn't *wait* to get married. You understand, of course. But then when we got home from our honeymoon, we started living life together, we blinked, and fifty years flew by! We now have a family of twenty-five precious souls spread out across three generations. In so short a time, our family grew from the two of us, to four children, who then married, and now the eight of them have presented us with fifteen grandchildren. That makes us a family of twenty-five. Just like that.

Stick with us here as we do the math out a bit further:

- Two people in the first generation
- Eight people in the second generation (our kids and their spouses)

- Fifteen grandchildren who, if most or all
  of them marry someday, become as many
  as thirty people in the third generation.
- Plus *their* kids? Our great-grandchildren?
  And *their* spouses? Who knows how big
  the fourth generation could be?

See how it adds up?

All we did was, we got married. Then, well, look what happened.

And if our family keeps growing at its present rate of acceleration, in ten generations these 1971 starry-eyed lovebirds will have multiplied to around 55,000 people—a city about the size of Sarasota, Florida. *And it's all our fault!*

We can't say to those 55,000 people, "We have nothing to do with you. Why do we owe you anything, sitting here where we live today?" No way! By God's grace, we can, we must, we will *think future*. All those people traceable to our marriage who will appear in this world according to God's plan—they will be facing unimaginable challenges in their time. They deserve, and they will need, all the prayer and all the help we can send on ahead.

The same goes for your family too.

Do you see now why we so confidently say, you really are a person of historic significance? And do you see why it starts changing how we all "do family" right now?

For example, our audacious prayer is that *the whole world will hear about Jesus through our family.* Ridiculous? Maybe. But maybe not, because when you consider God's greatness, *small* prayers are the truly ridiculous ones. We're not asking God for an *ideal* family. Not at all. (We surely aren't an ideal patriarch and matriarch!) We're just asking him for a *saved* family. We realize we're passing down our problems to future generations, same as everyone. But we believe in the grace of God. We believe it's through fallible but saved people—like us—that the whole world will hear about Jesus. Does he have any other kind of people to work with?

So we pray big prayers for our family. We believe it's true to God's big heart: to bless our family, and your family, and every family that turns to him. "For the promise is for you and for your children and for all who are far off, everyone whom the Lord our God calls to himself" (Acts 2:39).

> We believe it's true to God's big heart: to bless our family, and your family, and every family that turns to him.

We have found this way of thinking and praying and dreaming and caring to be energizing, invigorating. We find the true magnitude of our family and your family breathtaking, sobering, stretching, thrilling. In daily life, of course, our simple family routines are hardly impressive. We are boring! You too? But why not dare to believe that the future of the world is being shaped today through our Christian homes by the quiet grace of God? Nothing, no matter how ordinary, if it's consecrated to Christ, will ever go unused by the one who "works all things according to the counsel of his will." God *loves* to tell surprising family stories that will matter for a long time, even to the tenth generation!

Every time this long-term vision fills our hearts, it reminds us the family God has given us is worthy of our best, for the glory of Jesus.

So is yours.

How This Book Can Help

This book is not a family management guide. It is not a list of handy tips. It is not about self-help. We do hope you will gain insights here for guiding your family into their Christ-centered purpose, but we are not offering a fail-safe plan for family amazingness. God doesn't bless human grandiosity. But he sure does "give grace to the humble" (James 4:6). He pours his big grace into the ordinary lives we actually live. This book, we hope, will encourage you to believe it's true, and dare to live like it's true.

In a way, this book is an investment proposal. God is calling you to live your present life for the sake of your future family—and with an audacious faith in Christ they will be unable to ignore or forget. There are no guarantees, of course. You can't control the future, but you can invest in it. You can give your heart away to it. And as you do, you will be building a lasting spiritual legacy for the future, a future where you can already be living today.

John Paton (1824–1907) was raised in a devout family in Scotland. He became a missionary to the South Pacific islands now called Vanuatu. He courageously opposed the slave trade that was sinking the people into misery. It was not easy bringing the gospel of Jesus to Vanuatu.

One powerful help that kept him going, through it all, was memories of his godly parents. Paton described the day he left home, "launched upon the ocean of life," as he himself put it. It happened like this:

> My dear father walked with me the first six miles of the way. His counsels and tears and heavenly conversation on that parting journey are fresh in my heart as if it had been yesterday; and tears are on my cheeks as freely now as then, whenever memory steals me away to the scene. For the last half-mile or so we walked on together in almost unbroken silence. . . . His lips kept moving in silent prayers for me, and his tears fell fast when our eyes met each other in looks for which all speech was vain.

We halted on reaching the appointed parting place; he grasped my hand firmly for a minute in silence, and then solemnly and affectionately said, "God bless you, my son! Your father's God prosper you and keep you from all evil!"

Unable to say more, his lips kept moving in silent prayer; in tears we embraced, and parted. I ran off as fast as I could, and, when about to turn a corner in the road where he would lose sight of me, I looked back and saw him still standing with head uncovered where I had left him. Waving my hat in adieu, I was round the corner and out of sight in an instant. But my heart was too full and sore to carry me further, so I darted into the side of the road, and wept for a time. Then, rising up cautiously, I climbed the dyke to see if he yet stood where I had left him, and just at that moment I caught a glimpse of him climbing the dyke and looking out for me! He did not see me, and after he gazed eagerly in my direction for a while, he got down, turned his face towards home, . . . his heart, I felt sure, still rising in prayers for me. I watched through blinding tears, till his form faded from my gaze; and then, hastening on my way, vowed deeply and oft, by the help of God, to live and act so as never to grieve or dishonor such a father and mother as He had given me.[1]

Your children, too, will remember you. And they will be strengthened to keep following Jesus—to the tenth generation.

CHAPTER 2

Your God Is Better than You Imagined

*"For the promise is for you and for your
children and for all who are far off."*
Acts 2:39

Here's one reason we struggle to believe in the historic significance of our families: fear. We fear the future. It's scary and complicated. We fear we're too small for a challenge so big and bold.

Guess what? It's true. The future *is* too big for any of us to figure out. And we *are* too weak and unsteady ourselves. We're limited in every way from being able to force our will on other people, no matter how well-meaning our intentions, especially on generations we won't even be around to see.

But this dream doesn't die just because the challenges are bigger than we are.

The truth is, your family *is* significant—not in the eyes of this grandiose world, obviously. But the promises of God declare who you and your family really are. His grace resting upon your family is such a blessing as this world cannot give, or take, or even imagine. *How big God is matters more than how frightening the future is.*

Take his promise to Abraham, for example. Abraham and Sarah were childless. But God's promise included not only a future family but also a new "land" to possess and call their own (Gen. 15:1–7). And as the biblical story unfolds, God's promise grows. He promises to lead all his children not into a new land but into a "new heaven and a new earth"—a sparkling new universe forever (Rev. 21:1–5). God's promises just keep getting better and better.

It would be like if your dad promises to take you for your birthday anywhere you want to eat, anywhere in town. But then, on the big day, he ends up taking you and your family for a whole week to your favorite place in the world. That would be an amazing dad!

That's what our heavenly Father is like. He keeps being better to us—way better than we deserve, for sure. He never runs out of energy, love, and steady attentiveness toward us. He bears with us patiently, supports us faithfully, forgives us graciously, and provides for us generously. He's not tired of us today, and he won't get tired of our children tomorrow. Thanks to the perfect life and atoning death of Jesus, we and our children, to the tenth generation, can always open up the empty hands of faith to receive his fullness of "grace upon grace" (John 1:16). *That's the story God wants to tell through your family.* It's a story that keeps getting better as it goes along because *he* is the one writing it, *he* is the one doing it, better than we ever could.

On the one hand then, we can all agree that our world today and its outlook for tomorrow are discouraging, even bleak. This world is thirsty land and dry ground. Good news, though: God has promised to "pour water on the thirsty land, and streams on the dry ground." How? He does it by promising even better news: "I will pour my Spirit upon your offspring, and my blessing on your descendants" (Isa. 44:3). This is his twin strategy for infusing his refreshment into our desolation.

- One, he sends his blessing down *vertically*, in the moment, as people hear the gospel for the first time and put their trust in Jesus.
- Two, he sends his blessing forward *horizontally*, through time, as children in Christian families soak up the gospel at home and at church throughout their formative years, then are launched into life, bearing his Spirit into the future.

God's second strategy of blessing—the horizontal one—is what this book is about. As we shared in the previous chapter,

"The promise is for you *and for your children*" (Acts 2:39). We love that. Wondering about the future unknowns of life in this world, we Christian parents are not left bracing ourselves fearfully against what all might happen—social upheaval, economic meltdown, political extremism, family tragedy, worldwide pandemic, whatever. Yes, bad things are sure to come. But God's promised grace is *always* coming our way. He overrules the evil of this world every single day, bringing his good into our bad places (Gen. 50:20). In fact, the goodness of God is bending bad things around in the *opposite* direction.[1]

God himself, therefore, is all the hope we need for ourselves and our children, on into the far distant future. We don't need to wring our hands and "hope for the best." God has given us his assurances in writing, on the pages of our Bibles, come what may. "The secret things belong to the LORD our God, but the things that are revealed belong to us and to our children forever, that we may do all the words of this law" (Deut. 29:29). The Lord our God will always be there, bringing new life into a dying world through our Christian families, for Jesus's sake. Again, this promise is "for you" and "for your children" and "for all who are far off." Pretty good promise, right?

The Promise Is for You

God's gracious purpose starts with you and your family at your home, at your address. However modest your daily reality might seem, God Almighty is present there with you. He is investing spiritually in your family with an eye to distant generations, freeing you not to be intimidated by how bad society is trending or how small you are feeling. "The children of your servants shall dwell secure; their offspring shall be established before you" (Ps. 102:28). That's his commitment to the future. Such grace!

But the long-term power of your Christian family gets traction through *you.* "The promise is for you," the Scripture says first. Your family's future begins unfolding right now, with God's love for you and your love for him. You cannot give to your children any life you do not have living within yourself. Jesus can and must be real to you if you hope to send your kids into the future with their own spiritual reality.

The good news of the gospel starts here. Even before you embrace Christ, he embraces you, forms a covenant with you, and seals his promises to you. The Bible does not say, "The initiative lies with you." It says, "The promise is for you." All the best things in life start with him and his grace for the undeserving. We Christian parents can be so relieved! We don't activate a reluctant Christ for ourselves or our children. The active Christ keeps breathing new life into us—freely, endlessly.

His promise is for you, Dad. His promise is for you, Mom. "The friendship of the LORD is for those who fear him, and he makes known to them his covenant" (Ps. 25:14). Jesus wants to deal mercifully with you first, as your Friend, on his way to reaching your children as their Friend too. All you do is open up anew to him, fall into his arms, take all your failure and sin and leave it with him in his grace and mercy. That's how it works with Jesus—the only way it works. You give him nothing but your need, and he gives you nothing but his grace. True Christianity is always your ongoing openness to his endless grace. It's why the more floored you are by him, the more your children will feel his presence in your home and grow to love him the way you do.

> The greatest gift you can give your children is your sense of wonder that the real Jesus loves the real you.

The greatest gift you can give your children is your sense of wonder that the real Jesus loves the real you. Your amazement will rub off on your kids without your even trying. Stay humble, stay honest, stay amazed. The promises of God in the gospel are for *you*—first and foremost.

And for Your Children

We shouldn't be surprised at this—that God's promise is for us *and* for our children. "Those who fear the Lord are secure; he will be a refuge for their children" (Prov. 14:26 NLT). All through the Bible, our supernatural God works naturally through history and events, through people and their stories, and—of course—through parents and their children.

Jesus left no doubt how he felt about this. He *insisted* on blessing children, even pushing through adult resistance. He made clear the priority he places on the generation next in line, and he is equally intent on blessing children today. They matter to him. *Your children* matter to him. Here's why we can be so sure:

> They were bringing children to him that he might touch them, and the disciples rebuked them. But when Jesus saw it, he was indignant and said to them, "Let the children come to me; do not hinder them, for to such belongs the kingdom of God. Truly, I say to you, whoever does not receive the kingdom of God like a child shall not enter it." And he took them in his arms and blessed them, laying his hands on them. (Mark 10:13–16)

Our Lord acted boldly and emphatically, but also tenderly and gently. The Bible says they were bringing children to him "that he might touch them." But is that *all* Jesus did? No, he did more than they asked or imagined. He took those precious children up in his arms, he blessed them, he laid his hands on them. The tense of the verb "blessed" suggests that he blessed these children repeatedly, "fervently, in no perfunctory way," as one of our best commentators on the Gospel of Mark has noted.[2] His promise of blessing is for us *and for our children*—and he really means it.

Could we desire anything greater for our families today? The risen and living Jesus taking our children up in his arms, blessing them over and over, is what his mighty heart loves to do. The way he lingered over those children long ago, not hurrying but taking his time with them, and then explaining the beauty of what he was doing—it's a picture we should never surrender to our skepticism. Give yourself permission to believe these powerful words: "The promise is for you and for your children." Thank you, Lord. Count us in!

And for All Who Are Far Off

The love of God reaches far, in both distance and time. Your family, to the tenth generation, can participate in Christ's worldwide salvation. Those who are "far off" might not own a Bible or even have a Christian friend, but their need doesn't stop the Savior from reaching out to them. There are so many people, even far-off people, to whom he has made his saving promises, and he *will* get his gospel to them. He will use *your family* to reach them.

Maybe your children will become missionaries or preachers or evangelists themselves. Or maybe your children will stay and fund missionaries. Or maybe they will build a website for the gospel to leap over the border of a "closed country," where the good news of Jesus is not known. Maybe they'll write books that captivate future generations with the gospel. Or maybe start a movement to rescue children from human trafficking, or some other cruelty, for the glory of Christ. Christian families *will* do all these great things, plus a whole lot more, in future generations we will never see. And we don't have to master-mind these heroic future adventures. God alone is the great strategist. He alone knows the best way to make our lives count for his glory. Our part is simply to live each day consecrated to Christ, and *he* will make sure our lives matter, beyond "all that we ask or think" (Eph. 3:20).

Your children, serving him in whatever way he calls them to do it, will indeed make an impact to the furthest reaches of the earth, until the end of time. Everything done for Jesus pushes over dominoes that reach far beyond what we can see. He will *never* waste a life or a family or the future generations of a family who are devoted to him. "They shall not labor in vain or bear children for calamity, for they shall be the off-spring of the blessed of the Lord, and their descendants with them" (Isa. 65:23).

So let's be clear. *We* are not advancing God's mission. *God* is advancing his own mission, and we just want to be involved. He sees our hearts.

> Everything done for Jesus pushes over dominoes that reach far beyond what we can see.

He knows how it works best for each of us. All we need to do is follow him and teach our children to follow him, and he will keep his own plan moving *through us* into the generations to come. Let's keep saying yes to whatever he asks us to do. Could we live for any cause more worthy and more certain of success?

The encouraging fact is this. The risen Jesus is sprinting through our world today, right now, at this very moment, saving people right and left. He's not even tired, and he's not making it up as he goes. In eternity past he resolved upon this sacred commitment: "For the promise is for you and for your children and for all who are far off" (Acts 2:39). Our mighty Christ is why we aren't wringing our hands and moaning, "What's the world coming to?" Instead, we are rejoicing and declaring, "Look who has come to the world!" And when this world's terrifying possibilities get up in our faces to rattle us, here is our defiant answer:

> To those who ask, "What will happen to the world?" we answer, "His kingdom is coming." To those who ask, "What is before us?" we answer, "He, the King, stands before us." To those who ask, "What may we expect?" we answer, "We are not standing before a pathless wilderness of unfulfilled time, with a goal which no one would dare to predict; we are gazing upon our living Lord, our Judge and

Savior, who was dead and lives forevermore;
upon the one who has come and is coming
and who will reign forever. It may be that we
shall encounter affliction; yes, that must be if
we want to participate in him. But we know
his word, his royal word: "Be comforted. I
have overcome the world."[3]

In a world of so much upheaval, with so much uncertainty, and in families like yours and ours with so many real problems, "*he* will be the stability of your times, abundance of salvation, wisdom, and knowledge; the fear of the LORD is Zion's treasure" (Isa. 33:6).

Here is the biblical and audacious belief we are asking you to embrace:

God gave you your precious family
to play a crucial role in his strategy
for the redemption of the world.

He didn't give you this family just so they would become nice people who go to the right schools and get good jobs and don't mess up their lives too badly. No, he wants your family to become a prophetic presence making a statement in this dying world, bringing his presence into your neighborhood, into your whole social environment and beyond, to the ends of the earth. This is how, in real terms, God's promised blessing rolls on to the tenth generation. It's how the story of Jesus for broken people becomes the story your family tells, no matter how broken you feel today.

Yet it can start so simply—with a prayer like this:

Lord, I'm afraid for my family.
In this world there is so much against us.
But I look to you.
Your kingdom come, your will be done,
both in me and in my family,
to the tenth generation.
In the holy name of Christ.
Amen.

With this prayer in your heart and on your lips, your next move is not to go out and make a great future happen. Your next move is to *put your hope in God*. He will keep the promise he has made to "you" and "your children" and to "all who are far off." Then just start where you are, trust him for your next step, and get going. Your God is faithful.

CHAPTER 3

Your Marriage Says More than You Realize

"What therefore God has joined together . . ."
Matthew 19:6

This growing wedge of human beings entering history, your future family multiplying out to the tenth generation, will be here sooner than you expect, becoming more than you had in mind.

And you set it all in motion, which can mean only one thing: you are more significant than you thought.

So, what should you do, what can you do, with all this "historic significance" God has given you?

Hands down, the greatest gift you can pass along to your family is your own devotion to Jesus. As they see your love for him, they will know what it looks like to prevail over this world, and they will be better prepared for the hardships they will inevitably face. You don't give them this powerful advantage by being superhuman but just by being ordinary and staying true to Christ, by living a steady Christian life with a simple Christian faith—treating God as real, obeying the Bible, going to church, plowing your money into the kingdom, speaking up for what's right. Just basic Christianity. But what a gift!

Second greatest gift? This may be more of a surprise. *It's your marriage.* Why is that a close second? Because your marriage itself declares the gospel. Your marriage—yes, your imperfect marriage—is a prophetic statement from God himself, a sacred message he is embodying in you to share with your entire family.

Now maybe you didn't feel prophetic when you got married. You just fell in love, took your vows, and jumped into bed. Good! But something even better was happening. On your wedding day, there were not two but three people at the center of it all: the bride, the groom, and God. As the two of you were standing there during the ceremony, God himself was there, sealing and blessing your vows. It wasn't the pastor who joined you together. It was God. Everyone else in the room that day was merely a witness to what *he* was accomplishing, joining the two of you together as "one flesh."

Jesus himself explained marriage at this deeper level:

"Have you not read that he who created them from the beginning made them male and female, and said, 'Therefore a man shall leave his father and mother and hold fast to his wife, and the two shall become one flesh'? So they are no longer two but one flesh. *What therefore God has joined together*, let not man separate." (Matt. 19:4–6, emphasis added)

Your marriage is God planting the flag of his kingdom here in this world. He is declaring the gospel and building long-term blessing into your family's future—through you.

So here is an amazing reality this world would never tell you: *Your marriage has the touch of God upon it.* It is a miracle from above. Is your marriage perfect? No. Neither is ours. But flawed people are the very ones to whom God loves to give his miracles of grace.

In fact, when Jesus was teaching in Matthew 19, the topic he was addressing was not marriage at its best but rather a question about divorce. And what did he reveal there, even in speaking about the tragedies and heartbreaks that can injure marriages in this world? Jesus was saying that *your imperfect marriage today is as sacred as was the perfect marriage of Adam and Eve.*

Go back and read those verses again. Notice how our Lord is thinking. He looks back to the garden of Eden, he looks over at your address today, and in both places he sees the same glorious reality: "what therefore *God* has joined together." God joined Adam and Eve together, and God joined the two of you together as well, just as beautifully. No wonder Jesus adds, ". . . let not man separate." In other words, "Your marriage is your own personal garden of Eden. Guard your garden!"

Maybe you've been disappointed in marriage. In some ways, who *isn't* disappointed—and disappointing? But God values your marriage. He sees you two together as a precious treasure of his own making. So *marvel* today at your imperfect marriage. It says something about the God who joined you together. What really stands out are not your flaws; what's truly amazing is that no one less than God himself has been cherishing your marriage in his heart ever since your wedding day.

That's a living message the future generations must see and understand. Help them see it and be captivated by it in you.

How Your Marriage Can Bless the Future

But your marriage is not only sacred, *your marriage also makes a bold gospel statement to this world*. And the gospel, you can be sure, is the message God will faithfully declare throughout the coming generations of your family.

The Bible says marriage is both "profound" and a "mystery" (Eph. 5:32). That's not how this world sees our marriages. In all our fifty-plus years of marriage, no one has ever said, when meeting us as husband and wife, "Wait, you two are *married*? Wow, that's a profound mystery!" But what no one ever says to us, the Bible does say to us, and to you. Marriages are so common, so familiar, it's easy not to notice what's really going on. But Ephesians 5:22–33 gives us eyes to see how our ordinary marriages are declaring the profound mystery. Marriage is portraying the *romance* of the gospel—Jesus and his bride, united in love forever! That's the deep, lasting, and beautiful mystery *your* marriage reveals and displays. And your family gets a front-row seat to watch, in living color, your reenactment of the ultimate romance.[1]

Yes, the gospel is a story of *romance*, the love between Christ and his bride. And to show us the Eternal Marriage, to make it more real to us, God made us man and woman and gave us our momentary marriages.[2] He helps us embody this epic love story. So whatever else you may envision as being a reason or purpose for your marriage, here's the main one: your marriage portrays the gospel love story.

> Whatever else you may envision as being a reason or purpose for your marriage, here's the main one: your marriage portrays the gospel love story.

Sadly, our generation has lost confidence that manhood and womanhood really mean something. The confusion of future generations might sink into even deeper darkness.

But the gospel can always help us understand ourselves. It answers even basic questions like: How is a man a man, and not a woman? How is a woman a woman, and not a man? The Bible paints that picture for us. The gospel insight into manhood and womanhood is this: "It's not about difference *from* each other, but difference *for* each other."[3]

The romantic, euphoric love of a man and woman together is a major theme running through the entire Bible.[4] For example, the Song of Solomon is all about manhood and womanhood, each for the other, helping men be better men and helping women be better women. That's the point of Song of Solomon 8:6, the climactic moment in the whole book:

> Set me as a seal upon your heart, as a seal upon
> your arm, for love is as strong as death, pas-
> sion[5] is fierce as the grave. Its flashes are flashes
> of fire, the very flame of the LORD. (Song of
> Sol. 8:6)

In this verse, the bride is speaking to the groom. By marrying him, she has made herself vulnerable. She is pleading with him, basically saying, "Make me near and dear to yourself. Wear your wedding ring with pride. Keep our romance burning." Why? Because marriage costs us something. As with death, getting married means we lose someone—our single selves. So marriage is *powerful* in its finality, even though it's a death we gladly die. God himself set it up like this, filling romance with a fiery passion that sweeps us away. We *want* to belong to another, for the rest of our days, whatever the cost. But we long to know that the love of the one who has pursued us will last, the way *God's* love for us is certain to last. As the years go by and we start discovering how intense marriage really is—"the very flame of the LORD"—he burns away our selfishness to create a deeper beauty within us. God reveals something of the glory of his covenant love through our imperfect marriages. And our children watch us returning again and again to one another, keeping the romance alive. It's how a faithful marriage, even in the hard and rocky places—especially there—can help a whole family feel the warmth of *his* fire.

So now we're starting to see how the everyday dance of marriage, with all its nuances and subtleties of a man and a woman truly but imperfectly in love—that marriage really is a profound mystery. Each moment—no matter how plain, no matter how painful—is our next opportunity to invest in the future of our family, not by achieving perfection but by stepping into the grace of the gospel. It's the message that marriage is designed to declare. Here is that beauty, described in one verse: "To sum up, each one of you is to love his wife as himself, and the wife is to respect her husband" (Eph. 5:33 CSB). The more our marriages paint that picture, the more richly we bless our children who will carry this gospel mystery into the future.

A Husband's Love

Christ is the ultimate Husband. His love is lifting us into eternal splendor (Eph. 5:27), not making a more religious version of us, but making a whole new version of us, magnificent forever. This is our future as his bride. This is his love as our Husband.

This word *husband*, by the way, can also be a verb, meaning "to cultivate." For example, when Jesus said, "I am the true vine, and my Father is the *gardener*" (John 15:1 CSB, emphasis added), the old King James Version reads, "I am the true vine, and my Father is the *husbandman*." Being a *husband* means more than just "a married man." It means a married man cultivating and enriching his wife so that she flourishes, even as Jesus is taking us all into splendor above. That's why the Bible describes a loving husband as one who "nourishes and cherishes" his wife (Eph. 5:29). Her life is going somewhere beautiful and glorious, somewhere healthy and fulfilling. There's your goal, sir, as the *husband* of your wife.

Now let's just say, hypothetically, that you die first. Let's say your wife spends her final years as a widow. There she is, years from now, sitting in a rocking chair on a front porch somewhere, thinking back over your years together. And she's rejoicing: "What a great life the Lord gave us! We went through hard times. We made mistakes. But through it all, my husband thought of *me*. He put me ahead of himself. I feel so loved. If I could go back, I'd do it all over again!"

If you love your wife this way, your family will see Jesus in you. They will know how great marriage can be. And far more, they will know how great it is to follow Jesus all the way.

A Wife's Respect

The bride of Christ (the church) is the ultimate wife. And a Christian wife can put the gospel on display with beautiful power.

Your husband needs your respect. Back in Eden, God gave Adam a great task—to expand and guard the garden, "to work it and keep it" (Gen. 2:15). But a man can feel doubts gnawing at him: "Will I meet the challenge of my life? Will I climb that mountain God has set before me? Or am I a loser, as I often feel?" Your man needs the woman who knows him best to respect him most. Your respect can empower your husband to keep moving forward in God's difficult call upon his life.

This respect is a gift you give to your husband. He shouldn't need to earn it, just as you shouldn't need to earn his love. Affirm your husband. Speak well of him to family and friends. Praise him in your children's hearing. Your husband needs you on his side. Others will try to improve him, but in your eyes, he needs to be okay.

Both of us are still learning about love and respect in our own marriage, but one Sunday night years ago proved a real breakthrough for us. Ray was pastoring a large church . . .

———

. . . and he was crazy-busy. But on Sunday evenings he and I would debrief about that day of ministry. I always started with encouragements, of course. But then I'd share one or two "suggestions" that church members had given me to pass along to Ray. Of course, I thought I was only helping.

But on this particular night, after he'd heard as many of these secondhand upgrades as he could absorb, he took me in his arms, looked deep into my eyes, and said, "Darling, I need to share something with you. Every man needs one person who isn't trying to fix him, just one person who likes him the way he is. Would *you* be willing to be that person—for me?"

Boy, was I! So I decided right then and there: anyone with something to say to Ray could call the church office and make their own appointment. We wanted our marriage to be a safe place for Ray to love me and for me to respect him. I can't tell you how much good has trickled down to our family from that simple decision—to let our marriage reflect the gospel in a practical way. I'm grateful.

———

So again, we say, your devotion to Jesus is the absolute, number-one, most valuable inheritance you can pass down to your family. But this gentle dance between a sacrificial husband (like the Groom) and an affirming wife (like the bride) is the second-best gift you can give to your future family. It is costly. But it is worthy. It is of God.

Few sights in this world are as beautiful as an aging husband and wife still living for each other, by God's grace, for his glory. Your family needs and deserves to see this beauty in your marriage—even with its imperfections, every single one redeemed by God's grace.

> Your devotion to Jesus is the absolute, number-one, most valuable inheritance you can pass down to your family.

Remember, that's *the gospel at work in your home 24/7,* saying more to your family than all the preachers and teachers in the world.

In 1943, from his prison cell in Nazi Germany, Dietrich Bonhoeffer wrote a sermon for the wedding of his niece and her fiancé. He speaks to us today too:

> *God is guiding your marriage.* Marriage is more than your love for each other. It has a higher dignity and power, for it is God's holy ordinance, through which he wills to perpetuate the human race till the end of time. In your

love you see only your two selves in the world, but in marriage you are a link in the chain of the generations, which God causes to come and to pass away to his glory, and calls into his kingdom. In your love you see only the heaven of your happiness, but in marriage you are placed at a post of responsibility towards the world and mankind. Your love is your own private possession, but marriage is more than something personal—it is a status, an office. Just as it is the crown, and not merely the will to rule, that makes the king, so it is marriage, and not merely your love for each other, that joins you together in the sight of God and man. . . . *It is not your love that sustains the marriage, but from now on, the marriage that sustains your love.*[6]

Your marriage *so* matters—right now, and far into the future. Receive with fresh wonder the marriage God has given the two of you. And resolve today, right now—in *this* generation—to leave behind a legacy to inspire your future family, even to the tenth generation.

———

When I think of what laid a foundation for my walk with Christ, one of the things that stands out is how in my family, starting with my mom and dad and their marriage, Christ was a natural part of life. By this, I simply mean my parents made it natural to speak of Christ, to reflect on God's will, to pray, to apply Scripture to a difficult decision, and so forth. This is not something that can be faked or pressured. It's just the fruit of an authentic relationship with Christ that spills out into everyday life. It's what they were doing as a husband and wife, in their marriage together, and it became what we saw and experienced as a family.

I believe this is the greatest gift parents can give to their children: simply to walk with Christ yourself, simply to live it out together. Your kids will pick up on it, far more than any lessons you try to teach them.

Gavin Ortlund

PART II

In Your Home

CHAPTER 4

Making Your Home a Foretaste of Heaven

By wisdom a house is built, and by
understanding it is established; by
knowledge the rooms are filled with
all precious and pleasant riches.
Proverbs 24:3–4

As this big "to the tenth generation" vision for your family grabs your heart, you start thinking and dreaming and praying further out. We sure do. And that's great! That's part of what this way of thinking does for us all. The purposes of God enlarge our small categories. They're meant to. So let's dare to believe that the future is not limited to our capacities but is enlarged by God's promises.

If the first part of this book felt more like stretching our mental and spiritual muscles, this middle part is where we slip on our running shoes and start putting our faith into forward motion.

We'd call it practical, except saying it's "practical" makes it sound clunky and mechanical. We're not offering a method. God is too creative and personal for that.

Let's just say we're bringing it home—where God lives.

Who wouldn't love to be raised in a home like that, where "the rooms are filled with all precious and pleasant riches," the way Proverbs 24:3–4 paints the picture? Maybe not with fancy, expensive things, but with intangible riches like warmth, calm, sincerity, forgiveness, laughter, and gentle conversation. Such a home is not a lucky, three-point, mid-court shot. The Bible emphasizes that it's cultivated over time by the skill of "wisdom," the discernment of "understanding," and the insight of "knowledge." The wisdom of God can build that beauty in your home for future generations.

Some people are blessed to grow up in homes like that. Others grow up in homes that feel more like the bitter after-taste of hell than a sweet foretaste of heaven, homes where they are yelled at, belittled, humiliated, even abused. But none of us are stuck with repeating any past that fell short of comforting and affirming. Jesus *loves* to give new beginnings to wounded people, renewing us in the spirit of our minds (Eph. 4:23). And he *loves* to help us carry that renewal forward, creating homes that prepare our families for a better future.

Ray's dad was an example of this . . .

———

He grew up in a godly home, but in some ways, he told me, it was hard. For example, there literally wasn't enough room in the house for him, being the last of the five children. So he slept at the neighbor's house next door. It was the Great Depression of the 1930s. Times were hard. Families had to make do. His family did love him. But deep within, he grew up feeling like an outsider, always wondering if he really belonged.

On his wedding day in 1946, my dad resolved, "This new family of mine is going to be different!" He and my mom were so poor that they had to take a bus to their honeymoon in the Shenandoah Valley of Virginia. But sitting together on that Greyhound bus, they opened up and unburdened their hearts with each other about their longings for the future. That conversation was when my dad discovered in my mom, as they wept there, as they prayed there, the priceless gift of finally *belonging.* Right then and there, riding in that bus, God gave him a new beginning. And I can attest, as one of the kids in their family, all of us grew up in a home that truly was a foretaste of heaven. Imperfect? Yes. *But God was there.*

———

There's a good chance that maybe, for you, today is not as fresh and new as one of your honeymoon days. Special times and seasons like that don't come around very often. It's why they're special. But right now—this ordinary right now—can be your moment for committing to build a life-giving legacy for your future generations. These next few years in your home can tell a powerful story of the goodness of God in this world of disappointment. With all the other ways you might enrich your family for their distant future, one of the best is creating a culture in your home right now that overflows "with all precious and pleasant riches."

What is a culture? Basically, a culture is "just the way we do things around here"—the assumptions, the tone, the vibe of your family, flavored by the beliefs you revere together. And your family culture can prove to everyone who comes there, especially to your children who may still live there, how good it feels to belong, both to Jesus and to one another. We call this *gospel culture*. It flows out of gospel doctrine.

> A truly Christian family is one in which the gospel culture they share makes it almost feel like Jesus lives there too.

A family isn't Christian because they call themselves Christian. A truly Christian family is one in which the gospel culture they share makes it almost feel like Jesus lives there too. In an angry world where everyone is skating on thin ice, a gospel-culture family is a safe haven. A *Christian* home.

It can be *your* home.

Yes, it'll take some doing. A great home is no slapdash affair. A home that exudes gospel culture requires some thought. When we were a young dad and mom, here are some memories of how we thought it through for ourselves. And we know our train of thought might sound crazy. But, like you, we wanted a *great* experience for our family. So we literally asked each other the question, "What is ultimate reality? And how can our home be a place where we and our children experience that to the fullest?" That was our first step.

Our second step brought us closer to the answer. Here's how it dawned on us: In one of the best prayer requests anyone ever made, Moses asked God to "please show me your glory," and the Lord answered, "I will make all my goodness pass before you" (Exod. 33:18–19). So we started realizing this: we were raising our family in a universe where *ultimate reality is the glorious goodness of God.* It's a stunning claim when you think about it. But it's what the Bible says. It's what we believe.

From there, we took the next step. If ultimate reality is the glorious goodness of God, then how can we, the parents setting the tone of this young family, make it easy for our children to grow up believing that? How can our little home at 424 Bush Street, Mountain View, California, feel like God's glorious goodness isn't off at the other end of the universe but is right here in our living room, at our breakfast table, in the backyard? *That's gospel doctrine creating gospel culture for a family.*

So we started dreaming about how to bend *everything* in our home life toward reflecting God's glorious goodness. We didn't get radical, like C. S. Lewis, who said in a 1955 letter to a friend, "Far from having acquired a TV set, I've got rid of my wireless!"[1] (That is, his radio.) But we did, like Lewis, want to become decisive about the home environment we were providing for our children. So we focused, we simplified, we even had fun figuring it out. And it worked. But it wasn't us. God was there, leading us, just as you can count on him to lead you as well. "In every place where I cause my name to be remembered," he said, "I will come to you and bless you" (Exod. 20:24).

There's that "blessing" language again, the "how much more" heart of God.

Here then are two concrete specifics we commend to you for filling your home with "all precious and pleasant riches." They are well within reach.

1. Treasure God's Word

"Let the word of Christ dwell in you richly" (Col. 3:16). It doesn't say, "Let the word of Christ form a sidebar in your home occasionally." *Something* will occupy the sacred center of your family culture. *Something* will define what your home orbits around. If not the word of Christ, the Bible, then what? And why *that*? Only the word of Christ can enrich your family in ways that will still matter long into the future.

Ray can give you an example of this, from something that happened on his seventeenth birthday . . .

———

My parents gave me a new Bible that day. Here is what my dad had written in the front:

> Bud,
>
> Nothing could be greater than to have a son—a son who loves the Lord and walks with him. Your mother and I have found this Book our dearest treasure. We give it to you, and in doing so can give nothing greater. Be a student of the Bible, and your life will be full of blessing. We love you.
>
> Dad
> 9/7/66
> Phil. 1:6

I can still remember the first time I read those words. I guess people can write or say anything and act like they mean it, but I knew my dad really believed what he'd written there. He and my mom had proven it by how they treasured the Bible in their lives and in our home.

After reading his words, I opened my new Bible and turned to the verse my dad had cited. Here's what I found: "And I am sure of this, that he who began a good work in you will bring it to completion at the day of Jesus Christ." So encouraging! And so undeserved! I don't mind telling you, I was a total knucklehead back then, a high-school jock without a serious bone in my body. Rock and roll? Yes! Football? Yes! Jesus? Yeah, sure, whatever. But my parents' faith landed on me that day, knowing how the word of Christ really did dwell in them richly. And to this day, whenever I read this inscription, my heart still catches fire. You never know where or when your love for the Bible will have the same effect on your children, but I'm sure the day will come. I know how unforgettable that moment became for me.

———

Find ways to make it obvious that the Word of God is your dearest treasure. Children surrounded by reverence for the Bible may resist the gospel, even for years. But they cannot unsee the beauty you will show them. Be decisive about the Bible's place in your home. Make the Word of God an enriching presence in your family culture. The Lord will bless your family through it.

It can start as simply as this. Notice the two words on the cover: "Holy Bible." The word *holy* means sacred, set apart, *not* ordinary. Parents should teach their children to treat the book itself reverently because the *Holy* Bible calls for that. Children don't know this without being told and shown it. We had to teach our children. They were not allowed to toss a Bible carelessly or stack other books on top of it or use it as a coaster. If you will revere the Holy Bible and teach your children to revere the Holy Bible, your family will be better positioned to experience it as their dearest treasure in all this world. It truly is.

> Be decisive about the Bible's place in your home. Make the Word of God an enriching presence in your family culture.

Second, teach your children what you most love *in* the Bible—the good news of Jesus and his grace for sinners. The sweetness of the gospel message is why we often did our family Bible-reading over dessert. We wanted our children to associate God's Word with pleasure, even the sugar-induced kind! After all, Psalm 119:103 says, "How sweet are your words to my taste, sweeter than honey to my mouth!" Even now with our grandchildren, we might give them lollipops any time we're blessed to have devotions with them. We say, "This lollipop is sweet. And as you grow, God's Word will become even sweeter than candy to you. He is so good!"

When our children were young, we didn't have Bible time every night. We sometimes felt an early "tubby time" or a wild wrestling match with Daddy in the living room did more for our children's sense of the goodness of God than another after-dinner sit-down could do. Give yourself the freedom to decide on the fly what will best nurture a family culture of love for the gospel. But over the years, your love for the biblical gospel will come through loud and clear, and your children will love the Bible too. Like us, they'll always be drawn to things that give them *life*.

You may be thinking, *But where do I even begin? The Bible feels overwhelming! It's such a huge book. I don't know where to start.* But there are wonderful resources for family Bible time. For example, *The Jesus Storybook Bible* by Sally Lloyd-Jones is great for reading out loud, and utterly captivating—even for adults. As you read a Bible story to your children, the Lord will be planting seeds of curiosity in their hearts, sprouting into conversations later on.

There are so many other opportunities to consider:

- Dad and Mom can discuss together, at the dinner table or in the car, what they are discovering in their own Bible reading. It's another way to sow gospel seeds, as the children overhear the conversation.

- Explain before any Bible reading begins that there will be Skittles or M&Ms as rewards for correct answers to observation questions from the story.

- Pass around paper and crayons, inviting the children to draw a picture of the Bible story as they listen. Then afterwards they can share their drawings and explain what they liked best about the story.

- Set aside time during the summer for special Bible projects. Jani has done this for our grandchildren. She taught them the Ten Commandments, the Lord's Prayer, the heroes of the book of Judges, the Beatitudes, and more. "One generation shall commend your works to another" (Ps. 145:4). It's a major way the gospel culture in your family will deepen and last.

As our children matured, we upgraded our Bible reading approach. One year, when our children were teens, we took on a huge project. We wanted our teenagers to enter adulthood knowing that Christ could be their refuge all their lives: "In the fear of the LORD one has strong confidence, and his children will have a refuge" (Prov. 14:26). So we said to them, "Kids, what do you think of this? What if we memorize one verse from each book of the Bible this year? That's sixty-six verses. And if we can recite all sixty-six Bible verses from memory, we will take you to Disneyland!" They *loved* the idea! (We were planning on a trip to Disneyland anyway, but we didn't tell them that.)

Ray chose one key verse from each book of the Bible, and Jani wrote out each verse on a flip chart to help visually. Along the way, we kept bribing the children with treats, extra screen time, whatever it took. You know how that works! When sports or music lessons drew one or more of us away, we would meet individually with the children—Ray with one of our sons, Jani with our daughter. We'd bring the passage to read together, a question to get the conversation going, and then we'd close in prayer. You can imagine the excitement during the final weeks as Disneyland came nearer and nearer.

And we did it! All six of us helped one another reach our family goal, with the added bonus of enjoying many impromptu conversations about our verses along the way. What a happy celebration when at last we accomplished our goal!

Create your own strategies, way better than ours. But the point is, make the Bible the sacred center of your home. How else can you "tell to the coming generation the glorious deeds of the LORD, and his might, and the wonders that he has done" (Ps. 78:4)?

Looking back over our years as a young family, we see now that we made many mistakes. (*So* many mistakes.) But one thing we do not regret, not one tiny bit, is letting the word of Christ dwell among us richly. You won't regret it either. "Blessed is the man who fears the LORD, who greatly delights in his commandments! His offspring will be mighty in the land; the generation of the upright will be blessed" (Ps. 112:1–2).

———

I am immensely thankful for the family God gave me and the godly example my parents set. I'm especially grateful for the foundation they laid for us with respect to the Scripture. Both Dad and Mom were unyielding in their devotion to the Bible, reading it each day, quoting it to us, and living all of life with an obvious reverence for it.

Dane Ortlund

———

2. Treasure One Another

"Outdo one another in showing honor" (Rom. 12:10), the Bible says. What an uplifting, inspiring culture to build in a family! You can decide now to plant your flag right here: "As a family, believing in the glorious goodness of God, we're going to honor and enjoy and treasure one another!" Why not? Your family is a gift from above. God's grace is all over you. "The steadfast love of the LORD is from everlasting to everlasting on those who fear him, and his righteousness to children's children" (Ps. 103:17). Why not believe this about *your* family?

This brutal world can take the heart right out of us, can't it? It treats us like tiny components in a vast social machine. At best, it considers us useful. At worst, usable. Sadly, it can be as brutal to our children as it is to us. (Think of social media!)

But in our homes, how wonderfully different! We cherish our children deeply and tenderly. Each one is included and belongs in this place, simply because they're family.

No one else can treasure your children as meaningfully as you can. In fact, *you are the world's greatest experts on your children.* No one else on the face of the earth understands them as well as you do or cares about them as much as you do. You have been positioned by God himself to raise your children as no one else can or will, to be there every day with them, and to set a high tone of cheerful gratitude for everyone in your family.

> No one else can treasure your children as meaningfully as you can.

Typically, our children live with us for their first eighteen years or so. *Eighteen years!* Doing the dishes together, playing Connect 4, taking a walk, whatever. In all our doing with them, let's make sure we always place a high priority on making them feel wanted, to "outdo" each other in "showing honor" to our children. That's a gospel culture home. It is life-giving, not life-depleting. And in a world like this, what a glorious gift from God! It's a strong start on ten generations of changing the world through our families, simply by treasuring one another—one of God's sweetest commands for all of us to obey!

As a gospel culture family, we decided early on that, in our home, we parents wouldn't yell at each other, and we wouldn't let our children explode at us or at one another. Who wants to live in a screaming madhouse? We deeply resolved before God to live out before our children his beautiful command to "show kindness and mercy to one another" (Zech. 7:9). In our children's preschool years, Jani was careful to remember, "She opens her mouth with wisdom, and the teaching of kindness is on her tongue" (Prov. 31:26). Then she could train our little ones to be kinder than they might feel at the moment.

Children fight for basically two reasons. *One*, they are selfish, prompted by sinful hearts to demand their own way. *Two*, the grown-ups are weak, prone to give in and allow their children to vent their anger. Our natural tendency is to think, *They're just kids. They'll outgrow this.* But it is the parents' responsibility to set a higher tone for everyone in the home. The adults are the ones who understand how a *Christian* family behaves. It is wise when they set firm rules, because then everyone can relax and even flourish. We made it clear to our children: "Kindness is God's way. And it is our way. No matter how other families might behave, even other Christian families, here in the Ortlund home, we treat one another with kindness."

We modeled it, and we enforced it. We'd say, "Here is what it looks like to be kind to your brother right now. I know this is hard for you, so I will help you. But you may *not* be mean to him." If we saw a bad pattern developing, we'd enforce appropriate consequences until we saw a better pattern. But even in discipline, we tried to be as kind to the offender as the right outcome would allow. Charles Spurgeon, the British preacher, said it well: "When we have to do a severe thing, let us choose the tenderest manner."[2]

Here's the point we're getting at in this chapter. Jesus said that when he came, "the kingdom of *heaven*" came (Matt. 4:17). The kingdom of heaven is down here, where we all live. That's why we believe simple family life in all our homes can feel like a foretaste of heaven. Not that it's easy to accomplish. Creating such a refuge doesn't happen automatically. It's not just handed to us along with the keys to a new house. It takes moment-by-moment sacrifice. But a truly Christian home is so worth it. And the Lord has come here to help us all experience it.

Edith Schaeffer, a wise and bold voice in our parents' generation, said it bluntly: "Over and over again, *someone* in a relationship needs to consider the family as a career, a project, serious enough to be willing to be the one to 'scramble up over jagged rocks to feed the birds, so that they won't become extinct.'"[3]

Someone must take responsibility for this precious task, if it's going to happen. *Someone* must step up. The mother in your home might well be blessed with the privilege of making the family her lifework. She deserves the sincere respect and practical support of her husband, both Mom and Dad sacrificing to raise a family strong with gospel doctrine and sweet with gospel culture. Where else will children find a haven of protection from the assaults of this world? Your home, imperfect though it is, can be that shelter. Your home can be where troubled souls find peace, weary hearts find rest, hungry bodies find refreshment, lonely pilgrims find friendship, wounded spirits find healing, and a happy family shares laughter. Lots of laughter.

Why not ask God to help you make your home this foretaste of heaven? He will faithfully give you the wisdom, understanding, and knowledge you need. And you will fill your home with all the precious and pleasant riches of *the life that is truly life*—a glorious inheritance to enrich your future family.

Want proof? The convictions in this chapter, the vision that inspires our own hearts and has kept us going all these years—we received them from our parents.

———

My wife and I decided there were certain things we would have our children do and certain things they could not do. Some things would not contribute to their becoming godly people and as strong as they might be. So we just said, "Our children are not going to do those things."

I remember our teenagers saying to me at times, "But, Dad, all the kids are doing it! Even our friends at church are doing it!" Many times I said, "But you are not 'all the kids.' You are an Ortlund. This is the way Ortlunds live. We're not to sit in judgment of others; what they do is their own business. But this is *our* way of life." I believed God called us to certain standards that weren't necessarily the standards of other believers. When you have convictions about God's will for your family, hold to them. God can give you grace to claim your children for Christ.

I would like you to do two things. First, Mother and Dad, commit yourselves to Jesus on behalf of your children. Second, sit down and talk this whole thing through, what it means to claim every one of your children for Christ, what it means to guide your children and to expect their obedience. Start out with a reasonable plan with them, that they might walk with God. If your children resist, sit down with them, talk it over, saying, "We have a new course, a new way." Pray it through together.

God bless you.

Ray Ortlund Sr.[4]

CHAPTER 5

Parenting Today for a Confident Tomorrow

Direct your children onto the right path, and
when they are older, they will not leave it.
Proverbs 22:6 NLT

M ost days, parenting doesn't feel momentous. It never feels
prestigious. But the truth is, parenting has the power to
shape a child's destiny, and thus a family's destiny. John S. C.
Abbott's classic *The Mother at Home* declares it boldly:

> Mothers have as powerful an influence on
> the welfare of future generations as all other
> earthly causes combined.[1]

We think fathers belong in there too. Both Dad and Mom,
lovingly sacrificing for the long-term good of their future

family, will prove the deep wisdom of Proverbs 22:6—that being Dad and Mom keeps mattering far beyond those early parenting years.

This proverb is not a promise, not a guarantee, but an insight. Proverbs 22:6 is an elderly sage gently advising young dads and moms, "Your parental power for lasting good is *so great* that 'the right path' is really worth pursuing in the simple daily rhythms of your home." That's why this chapter is practical. You dads and moms have great power. God himself has given it to you, and he will help you follow through. Yes, your home life might not feel historic, but it has ten generations written all over it.

In this hope-filled spirit, we offer you eight insights that helped us direct our children "onto the right path." We hope these strategies help you too.

1. Study Your Child as an Individual

Child training works best when it matches each child's personal capacity. Pay close attention to your child. Engage him, talk with him, look deeply into his eyes, play with him, observe him thoughtfully. Notice, for example:

- Where is his character weakest and strongest?

- What is likely to lead him astray or keep him on the right path?
- What behaviors need your correction, and what deserves your praise?
- What *won't* he still be doing when he's sixteen? In other words, distinguish between childishness and character—thumb-sucking versus lying, for example. What habits will he leave behind and what traits might he carry into adulthood?

You will likely parent one child differently from another. With some kids, a stern look is all it takes to melt them into tears. With others, getting through to them requires more intensity and follow-through. But amid all the complexities of child-rearing, remember this and take heart: God gave your child to you, and he gave you to your child. He arranged it all. You are uniquely positioned to raise your child well. Enter into your calling confidently. By faith, accept—deeply accept—the demands of parenting your child into the adult God wants him or her to become. Rather than a fearful "What if?" let your spirit be a confident "Even if!"

> You're doing more good than you can see right now. You're making a deep difference that will last long into the future.

You're doing more good than you can see right now. You're making a deep difference that will last long into the future. The Lord will make sure of it. But for now, remember that each child is unique. Trust God to show you how to guide that uniqueness along "the right path." And he will be faithful to make your parenting impact even better than your purpose at the moment.

2. Be Careful Not to Crush Your Child's Spirit

Your child will need your correction many, many times, of course. None of us is born wise and virtuous. We all have to learn, often the hard way. But the Bible warns us parents: "Don't over-correct your children or make it difficult for them to obey the commandment. Bring them up with Christian teaching in Christian discipline" (Eph. 6:4 Phillips). Angry parental venting crushes a child's spirit. So does shaming a child into compliance.

Christian parenting looks like *Christ*. Does he correct us grown-ups? Yes. But does he belittle us? No. He dignifies us. Your goal in correcting your child is to represent Christ to your child, to correct him or her as Christ corrects you.

In the moment, of course, your discipline may hurt. But long-term, your intervention will shape your child's character, bearing "the peaceful fruit of righteousness to those who have been trained by it" (Heb. 12:11). And not intervening does no good for anybody.

Christian parenting combines wise gentleness with confident authority, which Christ provides moment by moment. Proverbs 23:13–14 advises parents to discipline promptly and early, because consistent discipline can make an eternal impact. A generational impact.

3. Teach Respect for People and Property

Jani's mom used to say to her children in their moments of conflict, "You don't have to love me, but you do have to respect me." Her mom stood up for what was right. And Jani did respect her. And that respect laid the foundation for Jani to love her mom deeply—long-term.

Teach your children to honor you even before they understand why it matters, because honor lasts long.

The fifth commandment says to all children, "Honor your father and your mother, that your days may be long in the land that the LORD your God is giving you" (Exod. 20:12). The whole reason this commandment is in the Bible is because God values life-giving, long-lasting family relationships. That's *how* intergenerational blessing moves forward. God loves seeing the bonds of honor, respect, and trust coming together to build family cohesion for the future. The fifth commandment is declaring it. That strength, that beauty, can be nurtured at your address, in your family. What makes it fruitful, by God's grace, is *both* the selfless integrity coming from the parents *and* the respectful honor coming from the children. When these two dynamics combine, great things happen.

The apostle Paul, in the New Testament, reinforced the fifth commandment as "the first commandment with a promise"—God's promise "that it may go well with you" (Eph. 6:2–3). In a home flavored with the gospel, the children honor their parents not out of fear of punishment but out of hope for happiness. Their lives will go better, long into the future, as they honor the godly example of their Christian parents. Honoring them means treating them as worthy, significant, and important, because God himself has placed them over the family. This kind of honor is practical enough to become second nature and long-lasting. Here is how a classic on the Ten Commandments says it:

> Solomon bowed down before his mother when he went to visit her, although by that time he had become king (1 Kings 2:19). Among us things are not so formal, but we may still expect children to show deference to their parents by their language and forms of address. Children must let their parents speak first, answer respectfully, be quiet when parents are speaking to them, say "thank you" when they receive something from them, and the like.[2]

The opposite of honoring parents, of course, is children insulting them, yelling at them, hitting them, or even just ignoring them. Dad and Mom, it's your responsibility not to allow those destructive follies into your home. It wouldn't be fair *to your children*. That's the wisdom of the fifth commandment.

Parents should teach their children to respect possessions too, both their own and those belonging to other people. Children are inexperienced in how real life works. They can easily damage precious things in someone's home, or pull glass jars off the grocery store shelves, or leave dirty handprints on walls. We parents are called by God to teach our children hands-off restraint, both at home and in other people's spaces, setting clear boundaries for expressing even innocent curiosity. Children who behave respectfully will be invited back into those neighbors' homes, enhancing everyone's experience of community.

A culture of honor is a big part of a family with a strong Christian future.

4. Require Obedience

Your child's obedience is not for your momentary convenience but for their lasting character. If a child is taught to obey his parents at home, he will be better positioned to obey God in adulthood. You stand in the place of God to your children—loving, teaching, providing, protecting. So when children defy their parents, they are defying God. When children are allowed to disobey their parents, they are being taught to disobey God too.

This is one of the key reasons why children obeying their parents "pleases the Lord" (Col. 3:20). You want the smile of God resting on your children their whole life long. It starts now, in your home.

How then can you nurture your child's respectful obedience? First, say yes to your child whenever you can! Depending on the kind of parenting that was modeled to you, this might not sound like the obvious approach for getting your kids to obey you. But think of it this way: our heavenly Father says yes to us many times every day. So ask yourself, "Why *not* say yes to my child in this moment?" Make "Yes!" your default response. It's what our Father does.

But, second, when you do say no, mean it, and stick with it. Your instructions are not the first bid in a negotiation process! Your home is where your children learn *obedience* as a sacred moral obligation before the all-holy God above. Often your response is a yes. But sometimes your no today is the best yes for tomorrow.

Obeying God only when we feel like it isn't really obedience, it's coincidence. It means a command of God just happens to line up with what we wanted anyway. Real obedience means following Christ even when his path is scary, unpopular, or hard. And if we expect that to make sense to our children for a lifetime, it has to start making sense while they're young enough to get used to it. Might they offer their input? Of course. But still, you make the final decision. And you will *bless* your children by requiring obedience. "Discipline your son, for there is hope; do not set your heart on putting him to death" (Prov. 19:18). A child who never has to say no to his selfish impulses is suffering the quiet destruction of his future moral character. But hearing a firm no and surviving the frustration of it builds endurance and patience way down deep.

Jani taught second grade for many years . . .

———

"Tommy" was a difficult student of mine with a reputation for disruptive defiance. He was also brilliant and enjoyed a challenge. So along with his mother—who wanted her intelligent son to succeed, of course—we formed a plan. We started him on a daily behavior chart. Every time I spotted Tommy keeping his hands to himself, working at his desk, or being faithful in any desirable behavior, I entered it as a positive mark on his chart. His goal was to earn 1,000 points by the last day of school. It required a lot of creative energy from me, but Tommy was worth it. And to my relieved surprise, he was making good progress.

Around midyear, it became clear what was motivating him. Me!

One day Tommy decided he would not obey his big 6'4" PE teacher. Each member of the class was being weighed as part of gym class that day. But Tommy refused to take off his shoes and get on the scale like the other children.

When I heard about it, after Tommy had returned to my classroom, I marched him back to the gym. With a few sparks flying, I demanded Tommy take off his shoes and get on the scale, which he did. What was the difference? When I asked him why he hadn't followed Mr. Dan's instructions and why he'd forced me to come down there away from my other students, Tommy replied, "I didn't think he would make me, but I knew you would." He knew Mrs. Ortlund said yes whenever she could. But when she said no, she meant it.[3]

———

We brought these same convictions into our home as well—convictions that helped us require obedience. It wasn't always easy in the moment. We weren't 100 percent successful at living up to our own standards. But we tried to be consistent.

For example, when a child was struggling to obey, we asked ourselves if our expectation was fair. If we determined the child *couldn't* obey, we helped them. We might say, "Are you so tired tonight? I know! What a long day it's been! You put away these three toys, and I'll do the rest." But if they put their foot down and *refused* to obey, that's when our parental authority went to another place. In those moments, we made sure that their disobedience felt worse to them than obedience. For example, "Either you give Eric's truck back to him, without throwing it, or I will give you a fifteen-minute time-out. You choose."

When confronting anger, we tried to discern the root of it in the moment. Was it coming from fatigue and low blood sugar, or was it coming from willfulness? Those are different kinds of childish anger, calling for different kinds of parental responses.

In it all, we gave many rewards. We tried to make obedience taste good and feel fun, or at least pleasant. We gave out stickers and sweets—whatever would cheer their hearts along the way. Enthusiasm sets an uplifting tone. And why not? God is good. We Christians believe this. It sure makes a difference in the everyday life of a home.

Children can and must learn that good and pleasure go together, just as evil and pain go together. Punishment helps a child feel the sorrow of sin, while rewards help them believe in the joy of obedience. If you keep making generous deposits in your child's "love bank," your relationship won't go bankrupt at those times when you do need to make a withdrawal through loving discipline.

5. Give Grace

"Requiring obedience" is tremendously important, obviously. But wherever our legitimate expectations become detached from grace, we might get the behavior we want in the moment, but will it achieve what we want for the future? For generations?

We really believe in this. Give grace to your disobedient child. After all, if you want your child to believe in God's grace, show them his grace. We're not saying to turn a blind eye. We're not saying to make excuses for your children when they disobey. We're just saying, before you take the hardest possible stance, consider the long-term power of showing unexpected grace.

For example, Rod Rosenbladt, a Lutheran minister, tells a great story about his father's grace toward him when he was a teenager. In a conversation with Steve Brown on the Key Life YouTube channel, Rod paints the picture:

> My dad gave me this old '53 Buick in high school. It was a straight-eight, which meant a long hood. And we had this high school fraternity. One night we were all drunk. I pulled out of this dark street, and because the car had such a long hood, by the time I could see, the hood was already out in the lane, and a Ford came and clipped me. My Buick fell apart on the street; the Ford only lost a headlight rim.
>
> I got to a phone and called my dad. I said, "Dad, I've just wrecked the car." He said, "Are you all okay?" I said, "Yes. There are five of

us, and we're drunk." He said, "Stay where you are. I'll come pick you up and get the car towed." And he did. He drove all those guys home, and then he drove us home.

First, he told my mother to leave us alone—a very wise move. We sat on the couch, and he put his arm around me. He asked, "What are you feeling?" And I was in tears. He would have had every right to ground me until 2075. But what he said was, "I think you need a new car. Why don't you go looking this week and see what you can find? And I'll take my lunch break and we'll get it." Those ten minutes made a theist out of me.[4]

Grace is powerful, isn't it? His father's grace was when Rod really started believing in God. If you want your children to really believe God is gracious, let them see his grace in you, especially when they *know* they don't deserve it.

> If you want your children to really believe God is gracious, let them see his grace in you.

Children eventually grow up and leave home, and the need to discipline them goes away—thankfully! But there must never be an end to the grace you show to your sometimes foolish child. How could there be? There is no end to God's grace toward you.

6. Teach Hard Work

Children learn their work ethic at home, and your example of diligence is the best instructor. Be today what you want your children to become tomorrow. Anglican bishop J. C. Ryle wisely advised us all, "Fathers and mothers, do not forget that children learn more by the eye than they do by the ear."[5]

We wanted our children to accept and even relish hard work. You desire the same for your children. And every child can become a helping member of the family team. Colossians 3:23 cheers us on, urging us to "work heartily, as for the Lord and not for men." Amazingly, the Lord delights in our work, receiving it as an offering to himself.

In our home we taught hard work in three steps:

1. When our children were little or were new to a task, we would perform the chore *for them* without asking them to do it. But they were present right there. We made sure they saw us performing the work cheerfully.

2. As they grew and became more capable, we would perform a task *with them participating*. This was the most frequent step. We might repeat it with them many times.

- "May I help you fold your laundry and get it put away neatly? Then you can get back to your book sooner."
- "I know you're anxious to get over to your friend's house. How about if I help you unload the dishwasher?"

3. Finally, as they became more responsible and we wanted to show our confidence in their growth, we would have them perform the task *alone*.

Work is not misery. Work is a welcome part of human dignity. Teaching hard work in these ways sets your children up for a lifetime of resourcefulness, resilience, and success. It builds a steady, forward-leaning, servant-minded maturity in their hearts. It invites God's blessing on their lives and your legacy.

7. Enjoy Free Play

Children learn by playing. Having fun is one way life can open up, more and more. And it starts by you having fun just being your child's parent! They will feel your joy as the life-giving flavor of their world. They will absorb it and join in, and will share the same joy with others.

Make it practical. Think through your typical week as a family, the ways your child might spend his time: sleeping, meals, day care or school, chores, family Bible time, church, music lessons. All those things are fine. Many of them are essential. But you must protect play as another essential.

The frantic pace of our world will eat away at your child's free play unless you put your foot down and say, "Maybe other families never stop to play, but we're different. We're going to do what we really believe in."

Undirected playtime creates a whole world of discovery and imagination. It's your child being free just to be a child, but also becoming better prepared for adult responsibilities without even realizing it. Yes, even play is a "tenth generation" strategy. For starters:

- climbing a jungle gym
- digging in the dirt
- learning to juggle
- looking for a four-leaf clover
- collecting stamps or coins
- building a snow fort or a tree house
- dreamily watching clouds float by while imagining the shapes they're making

These innocent joys help children's bodies grow strong, their minds stocked with happy memories, their awareness of the world enlarged, their thoughts lifted toward God and his creation and their place in it. Free play can also develop fine motor skills and cultivate problem-solving on their own. Free play stimulates their creativity and boosts their confidence.

And here is something from the musician and all-around genius Andrew Peterson that delighted us, with our own comment inserted:

> A teaspoon of garden soil contains hundreds of millions of microbes, which means that gardeners *[and children who play in the dirt!]* tend to have a wider variety of gut bacteria. One of those is called *mycobacterium vaccae* which, when it gets under your fingernails, releases serotonin in your system. Serotonin is a natural anti-depressant that also happens to strengthen our immune systems.[6]

So hooray for dirty children coming back into the house for a bath, cookies, and milk, with happy stories to tell of their wondrous adventures in the backyard!

Know what could make it even better? Go out there and play with them. Get down on their level and dig with their little shovel and pave a road for their cars and trucks. When you come inside, build with those blocks and set up the stuffed animal playground and help with that art project. Countless conversations might be missed if you don't, and lifelong memories can be made if you do—in addition to the health benefits of dirt under your fingernails!

For us, it meant buying toys that *we* wanted to play with as well. Our favorites were our Brio train set and a cartful of

Community Playthings building blocks. These investments seemed costly back then. But we have no regrets. And here we are, forty years later, watching our grandchildren enjoying these favorites all over again.

But play can be cheap too, like bubbles and balloons outside on a lovely day. Or on cold and rainy days, a warm bath and shaving cream on the shower wall, where little hands can draw and learn simple shapes, maybe even graduate to letters, maybe even start spelling words!

Perhaps consider doing one special activity each week, like a new floor puzzle or a simple science experiment. For us, making "play dough" together was always a hit. So was pulling out our dress-up box and getting into fun costumes. We "camped" indoors by making a tent with a blanket stretched between the couch and a chair, and then gathering books, pillows, flashlights, and a snack and just reading for a while. We don't even have space to describe our "Hide the Skittle" game, which children *love* to play. Everyone wins—and ends up on a sugar high!

Ordinary days with children can feel predictable, even monotonous. But ordinary days are vital in the development of a secure child. Why not make the ordinary enjoyable? Your children will feel

> Ordinary days are vital in the development of a secure child. Why not make the ordinary enjoyable?

loved. And as they grow, they will find it easy to believe God loves them.

Fun matters with teenagers too, as Ray's dad understood so well . . .

———

He was a busy pastor in California, serving a big church with heavy responsibilities. But I never wondered about his heart for me. Dad was in the stands at every high school football game, cheering more exuberantly than any other dad. He even came to many of my after-school practices, just standing on the sidelines, an encouraging presence.

When Dad felt he hadn't had enough personal time with me, he would ask me on a Sunday night, "Hey, Bud, want to skip school tomorrow and go to the beach with me?" Easy decision! So off we went, bodysurfing, talking, having a great day together. And when Dad wrote a note on Tuesday morning for the office at school, explaining my absence the day before, the school always marked it "Unexcused." But Dad didn't care. He loved his son. And I can tell you this: his son knew it, felt it.

———

8. Treasure Good Books

Unhurried reading, like your child just leafing through a book while stretched out on the living room floor—good books can enrich your family wonderfully.

God himself values books. He wrote one! And he is why we Christians value books. Your home can be a treasure trove of great books, leaving a profound impression on your children. Our son Eric, an author with a PhD who teaches at the graduate level, told us that the sheer number of books in our home during his boyhood made an enormous difference to him. Books can enrich a child's imagination and impart moral sensitivities. We urge you, make good books an obvious presence in your home.

Start reading to your child early on. Read before naptime. Read around the dinner table. Read before bedtime. Keep on reading to your child, and never stop. Develop your family library along the way. Maybe you have a room, or a corner of a room, where you can keep your family books. It can be a place of quiet, with no toys, where your children can enter new worlds opened by a magic key called a book.

God and his works are endlessly fascinating. There's always more to discover about our world and about the God who created and rules it. We believe parents enlarge their children's future by imparting curiosity about *everything*! If God created everything, then everything is fascinating, at some level. As your children launch into this lifetime of discovery, books will both answer their questions and stimulate their curiosity still further. A book engages all the senses in ways an electronic screen cannot. Who of us shares warm memories of our smartphones, the way we do about our favorite books? A great book may even be necessary to protect our souls from the destructive powers of technology.[7]

T. S. Eliot wrote of a book he respected, saying, "This is one of those books which ought to be studied by the young before their leisure has been lost and their capacity for thought destroyed."[8] We parents will not meekly stand aside as our children suffer such injury! We resolve, by God's grace, to create a healthy counterculture in our homes, where children can flourish, as they deserve to!

In addition to your family library, keep a basket of children's books near beds and favorite chairs, always within a child's reach. Help your children experience a worthy book as a joy. In our home, each little Ortie—every birthday, every Christmas—could count on receiving one age-appropriate book, a really nice edition, specially wrapped, then oohed and aahed over once opened. Good books invest richly in your family's future!

As you entice and enjoy and equip your children, building a God-honoring culture in your home, will you get tired sometimes? Of course. But your fatigue will be a beautiful offering to the One who "came not to be served but to serve" (Mark

10:45). Exhaustion for a task so worthy is meaningful, even satisfying. And when your weary heart needs a shot of fresh energy, 2 Corinthians 12:15 can reset your vision: "I will most gladly spend and be spent for your souls." Your precious children are those eternal souls. They deserve your cheerful best, with no self-pity, but only glad privilege.

Your most beautiful legacy is your selfless devotion to your future family. It's demanding, but their tomorrows are worth it all. Keep turning to the Lord moment by moment, trusting him for absolutely everything you need all the time. He is there for you. *He* is devoted to *you*. With the Lord of time and eternity as your constant helper, you can spend yourself for your family now, confident that through your heart will flow God's promises and purposes for them. Your children are going to need it, even to the tenth generation. And the time to begin, or begin again, is now—by God's grace, for his glory.

———

I have a vivid memory of snow billowing down outside the living room window of our house in Scotland. My father was studying at Aberdeen University; I was maybe six or seven. My dear mother had us three older kids sitting at the table with books open and she was reading to us, and helping us to read. I remember looking out the window at the snow, coming down so thickly, and thinking it was someone shaking feathers out of a pillow. I wasn't bored; I liked the snow, and I was perfectly content and happy to sit and read with Mom.

Reading has been really important to me—a doorway into a universe of ideas and trajectories, possibilities and dangers, glories and darknesses. It's been a major way to explore the world and a major way the gospel of God rescuing a dying world through grace and forgiveness has become compelling to me.

My father read to me growing up and talked constantly with me about what I was reading. But I think I associate reading more with my mother, with her at my side, hearing her voice as she read to me and with me. I was just old enough to be aware there were a lot of stresses in my parents' life at the time. But my mother was putting them all aside to read with me. I teach Old Testament at a seminary now, and my whole life is about that attentive, patient listening to the biblical text, and doing so with others. My mother was the first to do that with me. I've never been the same.

Eric Ortlund

CHAPTER 6

Seeing Your Family within a Larger Family

They feast on the abundance of your house.
Psalm 36:8

Y ou and your family, to have generational impact, will need support from beyond your family. God has kindly provided the very support you need, in your larger family called your church.

No one, and no family, can survive in isolation. Ray's dad warned us wisely: "To choose to be alone is to invite sure failure."[1] Simone Weil, the brilliant French thinker, made the same point in her own way: "To be rooted is perhaps the most important and least recognized need of the human soul."[2] So many people in our hyper-individualistic times have been uprooted. They were told they would be free by pulling away from others' influence and expectations. But now they feel lonely and afraid. Give your family the double advantage of deep rootedness, both in your own family and in God's larger family, conveniently available at your local church.

Your church doesn't have to be ideal. In fact, let's say it bluntly. Your church is *not* ideal. Neither is ours. We all know this. But it's better this way. It's better if it isn't ideal. Then it can be real.

You don't have to be in a leadership position there either. But if you'll just show up faithfully, Sunday after Sunday, year after year, deeply immersing your family in that community of God's grace, what a rich investment you'll be making in the future! You'll be positioning the coming generations of your family right where God's blessings are the most abundant in all this world. Good thing, too, because your future family is going to need all the blessing they can get—not moderate blessing, but abundant blessing from far beyond this world!

The pressures of our age oppose a gospel-rich family lifestyle. We're swimming every day through an ocean of frantic hurry, nonstop distraction, and constant exhaustion. We consume social media, for example, not noticing we ourselves are being consumed by it. Political hysteria and sexual chaos are literally within arm's reach 24/7 on our smartphones. The deluge of toxicity could destroy our families. All the warning signs are real. But this too is real, and even more real: "He who is in you is greater than he who is in the world" (1 John 4:4). And with the help of a church where our great Savior dwells, we can raise our children in the life-giving community he has provided.

Our Lord's whole strategy throughout the ages has been a big family. The church family. And his mega-family doesn't make your nuclear family less important, shrinking your family to the vanishing point. Quite the opposite. By placing your family within God's larger family, he increases your family's reach and influence. He combines your significance with everyone else's significance, using his math that makes 1 + 1 = 10. Your children may not see it now, what your quiet, unimpressive belonging and praying and participating over time is doing. But you are locating them right where the risen Jesus is present, active, and easy to find: your church.

God has been growing his family for a long time—since the days of Abraham, around 2000 BC. This family has grown so big by now that it stretches all over the world. Remember the huge vision God gave Abraham?

> He brought him outside and said, "Look toward heaven, and number the stars, if you are able to number them." Then he said to him, "So shall your offspring be." (Gen. 15:5)

Even more, God's promised family—all of us together in Christ—will soon be gathered together in heaven above. What a reunion that will be!—"a great multitude that no one could number, from every nation, from all tribes and peoples and languages, standing before the throne and before the Lamb" (Rev. 7:9). Now we're getting closer to the true magnitude of God's glorious family, where you belong.

His family strategy means your own family is a perfect fit within his purposes and ways. Just as he gave you your marriage to be a living picture of the gospel, he also gave you your family to be living proof of the vast family miracle he is performing throughout the whole of history and around the world. Your church is where your smaller family connects with the larger family of God. So next Sunday morning, get in your car and drive down to where your family can be refilled with the vitality you need from his everlasting family— "the communion of saints," as the Apostles' Creed declares it. You need that. Your kids need it. Christ provides it. And it's how you can be preparing the way for people who won't even be here until ten generations from now, when they'll need God's family too.

> Your church is where your smaller family connects with the larger family of God.

———

We went to church every Sunday. I know, it sounds so basic, right? But here's the thing: up through eighth grade, I never felt like I was getting much out of church. I'm sure I was getting more than I realized, but I honestly didn't have a vibrant walk with Christ, and I didn't particularly love church. Then in ninth grade, everything suddenly clicked. We'd moved to a new church, and I got deeply involved in the youth group, and my spiritual life took off.

So my encouragement for parents is to keep bringing your children to church as faithfully as you can, regardless of whether you think it's making a difference. You never know when they'll have a light bulb moment.

Gavin Ortlund

For Your Children: It's Easy to Get Saved at Church

Children who grow up in church—what a privilege they receive! Churchgoing parents are raising their children where salvation is fully available, clearly explained, and repeatedly offered. In this dark world, that is nothing less than a miracle!

Every real conversion is a miracle, something Jesus called being "born again" (John 3:3–8). But your church is where God performs this supernatural work naturally, through ordinary people who love the gospel. Even if your church seems especially unimpressive, the advantage is still built in: "Fear not, *little flock*, for it is your Father's good pleasure to give *you* the kingdom" (Luke 12:32). Will your children see flaws in your church? Yes. Might they at times want to turn away? In their teen years, probably. But still, they will remember what they have seen: Jesus himself embodied in the faithful saints of your church.

It happened that way for Jani . . .

————

When I was a child, my family moved from Chicago to Minneapolis, where my mother discovered a child-friendly church, Lake Harriet Baptist Church, a few blocks away. Although not yet a believer, she began bringing my three siblings and me to church with her. Sunday after Sunday, month after month, Lake Harriet Baptist embraced my family. And over the course of eleven years, all six of us, including my initially resistant father, were solidly converted to Christ! The trajectory of a whole family was changed through the steady teaching of the Word and the loving attention of the saints.

And to this day, four families—all four families that grew from these four young children—are clearly standing for Christ and passing on their love for him to our next generations, thanks to the quietly powerful ministry of a most unimpressive church, where God worked miracles.

For You: It's Easy to Get Renewed at Church

Every day, we parents press hard through the headwinds of duties, demands, and distractions coming at us from all sides. Work, marriage, children, shopping, paying the bills, taking out the recycling, mowing the lawn, checking social media, and on it goes. A week flies by and blurs into the next, one month into the next, one year into the next. To stop, be still, and think beyond the next task on our to-do list is something we'll get around to doing later, always later. No wonder the modern sage Os Guinness has said that focused attention is our rarest commodity, and time is our most expensive luxury.[3] This frantic world will distract us to exhausted emptiness if we allow it. We sure don't want to come to the end, regretting the lost opportunities we can never get back.

But as we fight our way forward, God has provided an advantage for us parents too—just going to church every Sunday. Seen with clear eyes, your church is a God-given oasis. He has built into your weekly routine a way to get refocused and refreshed. Church is a rich resource for long-term steadiness disguised as a short trip down the road.

> Church is a rich resource for long-term steadiness disguised as a short trip down the road.

The Lord can use your church to help you, without your even noticing it. Let's say, for example, the preaching there is sometimes, well, less than captivating. Even so, a mediocre sermon can still get you thinking: *Hmmm, why did the pastor say it that way? I think this verse of Scripture is saying something else. It looks to me like . . .* Do you see what's happening in that moment? The sermon *is* engaging you. You're thinking the gospel through in a deeper way. You're not hindered but helped by a less-than-stellar sermon. And if you hadn't come to church that Sunday, you would've missed the insight the Lord snuck into your thoughts.

Isn't it just like him to flip a mediocre sermon into a timely blessing, by his grace? All you do is show up, and the Lord meets you there, making your church even better than it is. And there you are, refocused on him and ready to ramp up for another week in this world. Why not thank him? And make sure you never miss a Sunday?

Then toss in, for good measure, the songs, the prayers, the conversations with friends, the seminars and classes and studies and mission trips. Your church provides you with multilevel exposures to Jesus and his gospel every Sunday, plus more. It's not hard for your children to be saved at church, and it's not hard for you to be renewed at church. Most churches are not impressive, but our Lord moves toward the unimpressive. And wherever he is, that's where we keep coming alive—again and again.

What to Look for in a Church

Few of us stay in one church all our lives, the way people often used to do. When you do make a move, through a relocation or major life change or whatever else, what kind of church can make a lasting investment in your family's future?

First and foremost, read the attitude, the spirit, the heart of a church, and choose one that is marked by humility. "God opposes the proud but gives grace to the humble" (James 4:6) is a theme running throughout the Bible, from cover to cover. God insists on it.

When you're wondering where your family can experience God, here is the answer from God himself:

> Thus says the One who is high and lifted up, who inhabits eternity, whose name is Holy: "I dwell in the high and holy place, and also with him who is of a contrite and lowly spirit, to revive the spirit of the lowly, and to revive the heart of the contrite." (Isa. 57:15)

Where then can God be found? In two places. Way up high, where we cannot go, and way down low among the lowly and contrite, where we *can* go. But God is harder to find in places where everybody is pretty much okay already, where church on Sunday is just the place they go to upgrade their above-average lives to an even more enviable level. Some churches even cater to those who treat Jesus like the chaplain to their status quo. So how can they experience him as he really is?

Jesus said, "Blessed are the poor in spirit" (Matt. 5:3). He is why, and this is why, you can't go wrong with a faithful church that isn't impressed with itself. His blessing is there. And your better future is there, down in the low place where the poor in spirit flourish under his smile. Put your finger on the pulse of the church you are considering and get a feel for the *heart* of it all.

Second, make sure Jesus and his gospel stand out as being obviously central in the message of that church. If a church complicates the gospel with politics or any other human agenda, you should *run* from there to a clearly gospel-centered church. If God's people long ago put their idols inside the sacred temple of the Lord, as they did in Ezekiel 8, let's keep our eyes peeled for it today. The apostle John—such a realist!—concluded his first letter with this fatherly warning to us Christians: "Little children, keep yourselves from idols" (1 John 5:21).

The apostle Paul worried about the Corinthian church in this very way, and he said so in plain language:

> I feel a divine jealousy for you, since I betrothed you to one husband, to present you as a pure virgin to Christ. But I am afraid that as the serpent deceived Eve by his cunning, your thoughts will be led astray from *a sincere and pure devotion to Christ*. (2 Cor. 11:2–3)

You are never wrong to expect of a church "a sincere and pure devotion to Christ." But if you settle for a church that's flirting with any competing devotion, you will be sending your future family off into a wasteland of spiritual suffering, far from Jesus. So we'll say it flat-out: your family, to the tenth generation, will not be wrong to expect of *you* "a sincere and pure devotion to Christ." And they will honor your memory for it!

Third, your family will need healthy community, clearly marked by honest and gentle friendships. Look for loving warmth among the members of the church. "Behold, how good and pleasant it is when brothers dwell in unity!" (Ps. 133:1). And why is it so good and pleasant? "For *there* the LORD has commanded the blessing, *life* forevermore" (v. 3, emphasis added). What a great resource for your family in every generation—life-giving community in Christ!

But any church with a taste for controversy—so tragic, so life-depleting! The stories of revival warn us:

> It is an instructive and solemn fact, brought out in the history of more than one revival, that when a whole neighborhood had been well watered with the showers of grace, no drop of blessing has descended there where a spirit of controversy and strife had obtained a footing. The Spirit of God hovered around, but fled from the scene of discord as from a

> doomed region where his dove-like temper could find no resting-place. . . . No dwelling can be more distasteful, no vessel more unsuitable to him than a heart which delights itself with matters that provoke contention and strife.[4]

Remember this too. Even in times of unavoidable trouble at church, you can still give your family the beautiful gift of your own non-angry, calm, peaceable spirit. They will bless your memory as long as they live. "A harvest of righteousness is sown in peace by those who make peace" (James 3:18).

Fourth, look for a church that is boldly advancing the gospel, and get your family involved. A fearful church can kill your family's faith, but a brave church will stir your family's faith. Your heart for Jesus and for people who need him will naturally spill over from the place you worship to the place you live, and your family will feel it.

Your involvement in church can be basic. Romans 16 gives us a glimpse into the early church. The simple words that leap over the centuries and land on us today are "worked hard" (vv. 6, 12), "fellow worker" (v. 9) and "workers" (v. 12). Again, it's possible to get sidetracked at church with activities that don't really accomplish much. But if you worship at a church where 1) the spirit is humble, 2) the authentic, biblical gospel is front and center, 3) the relationships within the community are honest and healthy, and 4) the gospel is not just talked about but sets the agenda, you'll *want* to get to work with your big-family members there, and you'll want to get your children in on it too.

A scholar-friend of ours told us about some research he came across. It looked at how Christian families pass the faith down to the next generation. Why do some Christian young people grow up to live all-out for Christ while others drift away? This study found one factor that favored long-term vibrancy for Christ: Christian parents getting their children actively serving the Lord along with Dad and Mom. Boldness for Christ at a young age makes a lasting difference. Go find a church that will help you live that out, and never leave!

Make Sunday Morning the Best Morning of the Week

No one has to settle for a frustratingly chaotic Sunday morning. "Hey Mom, where are my shoes?" "Dad, do I have to wear that?" "But I *did* brush my teeth—I think!" Gulping down a hurried breakfast, rushing out the door, arriving late at church again—who enjoys that? Why not make Sunday morning fun? It's the Lord's Day! Make it the *best* day.

Here are four steps that might help:

Start Saturday evening

Maybe Saturday night could be your weekly family night. A fun game or a favorite movie together would make a great prize for everyone getting their clothes and shoes laid out for Sunday morning. When you say good night, let your children hear the warmth in your voice as you say, "I'm looking forward to church with you tomorrow!"

Make Sunday breakfast a special treat

We usually had cinnamon rolls and scrambled eggs. It was easy to fix, and the children enjoyed it. But whatever sugary, unhealthy, lip-smacking delicious breakfast your children will absolutely *love*, spoil them with it every Sunday. And share your gratitude for church as you say grace over that breakfast.

Express what you expect

On your way to church, tell the children one behavior you are going to look for: staying close to you in the parking lot, looking people in the eye and responding politely when they greet your family, sitting quietly during the sermon, or some courtesy that keeps standards and morale high.

Respond to what you see

On the way home—or even before, if possible—reward good behavior. "Here are two Skittles for speaking so kindly to Mrs. Peterson." "Honey, did you see how Buddy stopped running down the hallway when I called him? Don't you think he deserves an extra sticker on his Listening Chart?"

Come up with your own ideas that will best engage your family. The effort is so worth it. Be creative. Make it practical. Have fun. And let your children see the sparkle in your eye. They notice what their parents love. All their days, your children will remember your joy in the Lord. They will grow up knowing how it feels to "feast on the abundance of [God's] house" and "drink from the river of [his] delights" (Ps. 36:8). Then they will be strengthened to pass on to their own children the gladness of moving through life together with their big family, where God's felt presence is so real.

It takes a church to nurture a family for generational blessing. You don't need to go it alone. Your Lord is thinking way out into your family's future. That's why he gave you your church. Never miss a Sunday!

———

The healthiest part of family life growing up, now that I look back on it from my forties, was the natural and assumed commitment my parents made to the local church. Whatever the weather, whatever our mood, we were at church on Sundays. I'm grateful that when I left home at eighteen, this was normal to me.

Dane Ortlund

PART III

To the Generations

CHAPTER 7

The Best Gift for Your Grandchild

*"Arise, cry out in the night, at the beginning
of the night watches! Pour out your heart like
water before the presence of the Lord! Lift your
hands to him for the lives of your children."*
Lamentations 2:19

If God has given you the privilege of becoming a grandparent, you are blessed with a relationship like no other. And through that special relationship, you are already strengthening your family for a distant future long after you've left this world.

One recent summer, for example, we got our whole family together in Nashville for five days of off-the-charts fun. Since our kids, spouses, and children are scattered so far across the country, even *out* of the country, it was the first time all of us had been together in this configuration, in one place . . . ever. Several of our grandkids had never met each other in person.

We paid everyone's way here and back, put them up at the Gaylord Opryland Resort, and called it Our Family Gathering. (Clever!) And it really was fun. The water park, the games, the jokes, the great food—we had a *blast*. Officially, it was a celebration of our fiftieth wedding anniversary. But the two of us had even greater plans in mind for what we'd be celebrating during that week.

Here's the backstory to it.

In 2007, when Ray's saintly father died, his funeral became a defining moment for us and our adult children. It marked all of us together as *a Christian family*. We already were, of course, but we just went deeper. "Grandpa's devotion to Jesus," we remember thinking and saying to one another, "that's who *we* are too, down to our core. That's our family, and we wouldn't want to live any other way." We knew we had a sacred treasure to prize and to hand down to our future family.

So in 2023, on this happier occasion, we longed and prayed for *our grandchildren* to have that same kind of "aha" moment for their future too. Our Family Gathering was designed to treat them to a special experience of what it means to be "us"—a family in Christ.

In fact, here's what we wrote on the front page of a little booklet we put together for the occasion. We had it printed

and bound at a local business supply dealer, and we handed it
out to everyone as our guide to the week:

> Mayme and Bapa welcome you! We are *over-joyed* that you are with us! We have been pray-
> ing and preparing for Our Family Gathering
> for a long time. Now at last, we are here
> together. Thank you for coming.
>
> The Lord Jesus has been so kind through-
> out our fifty-plus years of marriage. He has
> been attentive, patient, forgiving, protective,
> and present every day. We are praising him
> for the past, and we are trusting him for the
> future—*your future.*
>
> Here is the Scripture that stirs our hearts
> for these precious days together:
>
> One generation shall commend your
> works to another, and shall declare your
> mighty acts. (Ps. 145:4)
>
> We are praying that we, in our genera-
> tion of this family, will commend our Lord's
> mighty acts to your two generations. What
> greater treasure could we give you for you to
> pass on to future generations? We are praying
> that Our Family Gathering 2023 will enrich
> all of us in the gospel of Christ, with his living

presence felt even to the tenth generation!
Thank you for joining us in that vision and
expectancy.

With all our love,
Mayme and Bapa

In later pages, we shared a few of the high points in each
of our histories, first as kids, then as a couple, then as a family
(complete with pictures)! We included everyone's anniversary
dates and birthdays as a keepsake reference, along with a flex-
ible but also intentional agenda for the week ahead, as well as
lyrics to some of the worship songs we wanted to share and
learn as a family together.

And apparently, by God's grace, Our Family Gathering
worked! Here's what our oldest granddaughter listed as her big-
gest takeaways from the week:

- Family supports family; we share our
  struggles and joys honestly
- A clear sense of family direction, like the
  Heidelberg Catechism, Question 1
- Each grandchild receiving a Bible showed
  that faith in Christ is *shared* among us

We asked our next oldest, a grandson, what stood out to
him too. Here's his list:

- How important it is to honor and encourage one another
- It is comforting not to be alone in life
- When we're going through hard times, our family is on our side

What also struck us is what *no one* said. No one in the family talked about money or career or politics as defining issues among us. Our focus on Jesus pushed lesser things away and brought the most precious things very near—within our reach, to cherish forever.[1]

As you can imagine, we came away from this experience even closer to each of our grandchildren and even more thankful for the privilege of being their grandparents.

We realize, of course, you may not yet *be* a grandparent. But this chapter is still for you. Now is the right time to start thinking ahead about the grandparent you'll one day become. There's value, too, in looking for ways to encourage your own children's grandparents (your parents) in the here and now. This "tenth generation" vision, mentality, and way of life helps you see yourself beyond your right-now experience. This crucial chapter, if it doesn't speak your language in the moment, will still help you get ready for your grandparenting future.

Will you stay with us then? For just a minute?

Being a grandparent means discovering, almost beyond belief, that you can love another child or children as dearly as

TO THE TENTH GENERATION

you loved your own kids. It also means feeling some regrets about how you did as a parent yourself. Maybe you wish you'd grasped the treasure of those years, the way you see them more clearly now. Oh, the things we'd all do differently if given another chance!

But your regrets show how much you've grown. Way to go! Now, by God's grace, you have something deeper to give away. All these years, through the ups and downs, the Lord has been with you, investing in you. Now you're ready for your future, even more ready than if you'd somehow been a Perfect Parent from the start.

> Now you're ready for your future, even more ready than if you'd somehow been a Perfect Parent from the start.

What we're trying to learn is how best to share the richer, deeper blessings of our years as grandparents. And if your situation is anything like ours, part of the challenge comes from living at a great geographical distance from your grandchildren. In our twenty years of grandparenthood (did we just invent a new word?), we've never lived closer than five hundred miles to any of our grandchildren. How did that happen? Well, we raised our children to think for themselves and follow Jesus wherever he leads—and then they did! The distances make our visits too infrequent and brief for our liking.

But it's okay. We do want to give them all we can, but we don't *need* to be there constantly. The Lord is with our entire family all the time, and he is better at caring for them than we are. Look how relaxed the apostle Paul, a spiritual patriarch, seemed to feel toward a church he deeply loved, the way we love our grandkids:

> My dear friends, as you have always obeyed—not only in my presence, but now much more in my absence—continue to work out your salvation with fear and trembling, for it is God who works in you to will and to act in order to fulfill his good purpose. (Phil. 2:12–13 NIV)

In other words, "I miss you, but you don't need me there. I don't have to be the one to answer all your questions and solve all your problems. God himself is there with you. In fact, he is working *within* you. So look to him, think things through, and you will find your way. You're in his good hands!"

Such wisdom! Paul loved them, but he wasn't controlling them. He trusted the Lord for them. Yes, he was deeply committed to them. But he was also free, and so were they. Look how he wisely combined two dynamics: 1) he gave them away to Christ, and 2) he cheered them on in Christ. Would they be perfect? No. Would they sin and suffer losses and shed tears of regret sometimes? Yes. But would the Lord be with them through it all? Yes. And Paul would encourage and pray for them until his dying day, even as you encourage and pray for your family today—and you always will, until your dying day.

That's the best gift you can give to your grandchildren: your confidence in the God who is with them when you can't be.

Thinking about your family future-tense and long-term, clearly your most important investment in them is your own confidence in God. Your days of direct parenting may be over, but your steady trust in God will nurture the up-and-coming generations in their own trust in God. That's a parental and grandparental priority you can and must continue. You're not done yet. Far from it! The longer you live, and especially the more you suffer, your example of trusting the Lord, come what may; your example of praying, without ceasing; your example of treating Jesus as real, when it counts—these are *powerful* blessings you can pass down to your children and grandchildren, and on to the tenth generation.

Your faithful prayers, in fact, are so dear to our Lord that he includes them in his very identity. Look how he invites us to address him: "O you who hear prayer . . ." (Ps. 65:2). He is your prayer-hearing, prayer-answering God. He is your confidence always—not how well *you* pray, but simply who *he* is. He is strong when you are weak. He is present when you are absent. He is wise when you are overwhelmed. Amazingly, "God fixes our prayers on the way up. If he does not answer the prayer we made, he will answer the prayer we should have made."[2] And *he* is the one shepherding your family now and into the distant future.

Best of all, he can win the hearts of your family, both present and future, by his grace in Jesus Christ.

That's why your sense of *who God is in his grace and mercy to you*—this heart-level awareness is the greatest gift you can pass down to them. Here's how wonderful it can be. Your unseen presence will long be felt in the future generations of your family, as God answers your prayers offered today. So tell him your longings, your fears, your hopes. Pour it out. Wherever you are, whenever you are—*pray!*—then pray some more, everywhere and always, for those dear to you! God, Almighty God, who delights in your prayers, will hear you, cherish you, and answer you. God never lets your faith go unmet.

> Wherever you are, whenever you are—*pray!*—then pray some more, everywhere and always, for those dear to you!

Very soon these grandchildren of yours will begin their own families, and on and on, to ten generations. Let's not fear the future they will be facing. Let's not worry about the downward spiral of history. Trends are always frightening. But Jesus said, "All authority in heaven and on earth is given to me" (Matt. 28:18). *Everything is going his way!* As Paul Johnson, the great historian of the twentieth century, helps us see:

> What is important in history is not only the events that occur but the events that obstinately do not occur. The outstanding non-event of modern times was the failure of religious belief to disappear.[3]

Do not be disheartened by the bluff and the saber-rattling of this angry world. High above the melodrama of this soap opera called history, *Jesus reigns.* And he is yours, and you are his, and he cares deeply about everyone you care about. As your heart feels and even breaks for those you love, your broken heart enters into the heart of the Lord. *You* go to a deeper place with him, feeling what he himself feels. The first person in your family to be blessed by your prayers is you. But you are not the last, for sure! He will receive your prayer, and he will send down his blessing—starting with you, and continuing through your children and grandchildren.

———

I believe this so strongly myself—Jani, as a grandmother—I've dedicated a page for each grandchild in my prayer notebook. When we visit a particular part of our family, I often show a grandchild his or her page, complete with prayer requests and favorite photos. Then, when they know how to write, I ask them to sign their page and date it. Those prayer pages are building strong family bonds that, by God's grace, will last long into the future.

Here, in fact, are some of those prayers, saturated with the very words and phrases of Scripture, that you might find meaningful as you pray over your own family. Maybe you'd like to underline or highlight the parts that resonate the most.

A Prayer for Your Granddaughter

O Father God,

Thank you for this little girl. We receive her as a gift from you. We ask that from a young age she would claim you as the only true God, and her God. Open the eyes of her heart to know and love Jesus Christ as her personal Savior. May she be as fearless as Sarah, as loyal as Ruth, as discerning as Abigail, as faith-filled as Mary.

Help her to store up your Word in her heart, keeping her from sin and folly. Set her heart free to love going to church every week, and let her flourish there among your holy people. Keep her from being wise in her own eyes or leaning on her own understanding. When her soul is searching for happiness and security, help her to find her rest in Christ alone. Give her the grace to prize your wisdom and instruction above all earthly treasures.

As her body grows into lovely womanhood, impart to her the imperishable beauty of a gentle and quiet spirit, so precious in your sight. May she stand like a corner pillar cut for a palace, living a life of saintly nobility.

Protect her and her future husband from sexual confusion. So preserve them, that they may enter marriage free from shameful memories and painful regrets. If they stray, bring them back to a deeper sense of your grace for the undeserving. Let their marriage be one of vows kept and hopes fulfilled.

Give our granddaughter a man who loves you with all his heart, one who will nourish and cherish her even as you do your bride. Help her to do him good all the days of her life. Clothe her with strength and dignity as she looks well to the ways of her household, making her home a foretaste of heaven.

When you bless her with children, open her mouth day by day to tell them the wonders you have done, so that they set their hope in you. May her love for you inspire her family.

O Father, take this little girl and build her into a mighty woman of God, for your kingdom's sake. Grow her faith into a generational faith. Pour your Spirit upon me, so that the gospel she hears from me will pass down to her children and her children's children. Then bring us all together around your throne, united forever in your love for us and our love for you.

In Jesus's name. Amen.

A Prayer for Your Grandson

O Father God,

Thank you for this little boy. We receive him as a gift from you. Be his God from his earliest days, all the way until his final breath in this world. Open his heart to receive the abundance of grace and the free gift of righteousness you offer in your Son Jesus Christ. Pour out your Spirit upon him in abundant measure. Let him claim you with bold-hearted clarity, declaring for all to hear, "I am the Lord's!"

May his conduct always be in step with the truth of the gospel. Nurture within his soul an appetite for wisdom as the sweetest taste. Let him know and feel how satisfying you are, beyond all this world can offer. Fill him with spiritual power. Set him apart with biblical integrity at all times, in all circumstances.

Make him a David in his generation, useful in your service. Give him the courage of his elder brother, Jesus, to fight the battles you call him to. Grow him into a valiant warrior. Let his speech be wise and engaging. Make him a man of good presence, representing you faithfully to his generation.

Develop in him the excellence of a Daniel—of good appearance, skillful in all wisdom. Train and qualify him to stand in places of leadership. Make him fearless in speaking for you, redirecting all praise from himself to your glory.

Give him a happy heart, blessing you with all the enthusiasm that is within him. Protect and defend him against impurity of heart or hands. Give him close brothers to encourage him along the way, and whom he can encourage, toward a life marked by your truth.

Give him the humility to consider rebukes rather than scorn them. Temper his natural defensiveness with a willingness to listen and learn. Shape him into a man others can trust and respect. Strengthen him to reject sin and folly, however stylish they may be in this world. Lift him up as a prince in all the earth.

Preserve him from sexual confusion. Protect and prepare his wife as she grows up. Bring them together with true romance, give them a shared heart for Christ, and establish their children in the gospel. May the truths he hears from my mouth leave such an impression that they will be heard by his children from his own mouth, and on to the tenth generation. And when his father and mother come to die, stand by him yourself, so that he carries on your work ever faithfully.

In Jesus's name. Amen.

A Prayer for Your Married Children

O Father God,

We thank you for this marriage. We honor it as a gift from above. Now keep this man and this woman together with a love as strong as death. Sustain them as they fulfill the sacred vows they made in your presence on their wedding day. Show our daughter how to respect her husband, how to do him good all the days of their life together. And show our son how to love his wife selflessly, how to live with her in an understanding way that touches her heart. Grant that, together as one, they may faithfully love, honor, and cherish each other in true godliness as long as they both shall live.

Refresh their romance along the way with delightful passion. Keep any root of bitterness far away. Strengthen them when they are weary, and comfort them when they are sad. Grant that your peace will fill their home, making it a very foretaste of heaven.

Guide them as they raise their children. Help them to pass on, in word and deed, a clear vision of wholehearted devotion to Christ, so that our grandchildren grow up with an attractive example to follow. Impart to this husband and wife the wisdom needed to instruct their children in all that is good and lovely. And give our dear children the steadfast courage to lead our grandchildren in the paths of righteousness, sustained by the strong promises of your Word.

Preserve this family here on earth, and reunite us all around your throne above, we earnestly pray.

In Jesus's name. Amen.

A Prayer for Your Family to the Tenth Generation

O Father God,

Here we are, in your story, by your grace, for your glory.

Now what shall we say? How shall we pray?

Above all else, we beg you to pour your Spirit out upon our offspring and your blessing on our descendants, so that we will all claim the

Lord Jesus Christ as our own. Save us from sin, and give us new hearts, so that we love the Lord our God joyously, taking our stand for Christ with courage and integrity in each generation.

Help us, each one, to believe, love, know, and obey the Bible. Make your Word sweet to our taste. Guide our feet along your paths, desiring and doing what is fully pleasing to you. Win our hearts, so that we hold fast to you, losing all things in order to gain Christ. Help us to always set our hope in you, keeping your commandments, never forgetting your works.

May our descendants be known among the nations, so that many see your glory in them. May your kingdom come, may your will be done, through this family. In the place of their fathers, make the sons of this family like princes in all the earth, leaders in their generation. Make our daughters like corner pillars, cut for the structure of a palace—strong and beautiful supports for their families.

Dwell in such a way with each generation of our family that they gladly pass on the gospel to the next generation, fearing you and serving you faithfully with all their heart, as they consider what great things you have done for them.

Help everyone born to this family, to the tenth generation, conquer Satan by the blood of the Lamb and by the word of their testimony, not loving their lives even unto death. May we follow the Lamb wherever he goes, all the way, until we see your face, O our gracious King.

For your greater glory and our endless joy.

In Jesus's name. Amen.

———

We are called on as parents and grandparents and friends of those who have children to protect those little ones, not by building fear into them but by building faith into them. The parents of Moses, the Bible says, were "not afraid" (Heb. 11:23). I don't think the attitude of the Christian parent should be fear of what this harsh and vulgar world is going to do to them, but faith that God has given to us a precious life to claim for Christ. We don't live cowering in fear. Your child, your grandchild, belongs to God.

Ray Ortlund Sr.[4]

CHAPTER 8

When Family Feels like a Failure

*. . . in order that, just as Christ was raised
from the dead by the glory of the Father,
we too might walk in newness of life.*
Romans 6:4

Every family sins. Every family suffers for it. Every family needs new beginnings along the way. Your hope for your future family is not found in your perfect performance. Your hope is in Christ, and our hope is in Christ. He is the only Savior of all our families, including those who seem to be doing it perfectly.

The truth is, we *all* need the very thing the gospel so clearly promises: God's grace for the undeserving. It's what keeps our chins above water every day. We don't deserve his blessing, but

Jesus did all the deserving for us. All we do, all we *can* do, is receive his grace with the empty hands of faith.

A family getting a fresh start together by his grace—we aren't saying it's easy. We certainly have no formulaic answers for complicated problems. But we do know this: *God is gracious.* Our sins do real damage to our families, but God's grace means these failures do not doom our families. Deep regrets are not a death blow. We have hope. But our only hope is to put all our hope in the grace of God.

> All we do, all we *can* do, is receive his grace with the empty hands of faith.

What is the grace of God? Back in the Old Testament, the word translated "grace" suggests the idea of doing something "for no reason." For example, this word shows up when King Saul opposed young David "for no reason" (1 Sam. 19:5 NIV). David had given Saul no reason for hating him. The king just hated David—for his own reasons. Okay, let's turn that concept around, making the sneer into a smile, and let's look at it again. *Why* does God love you? For no reason—no reason in you, anyway. The reason is just because he loves you—period. All the reasons, motivations, and inducements God needs for loving you are within God himself. You don't need to make him keep loving you by inspiring him with your model behavior.

His heart moves toward you in kindness for reasons you can neither deserve nor defeat. God *is* love (1 John 4:16).

Here's how big God's grace is. Think of a big banner stretched out wide over your family, stretching from here all the way to the tenth generation. It's huge. It's grand. Now imagine the following words written clearly and beautifully on that banner: "to the praise of his glorious grace" (Eph. 1:6). *That big grace is your big hope for your future family.* Will they be impressive in this world's eyes? Maybe, maybe not. But here is what God can show the world when they look at your family. Not a perfect family but a saved family, saved not just by his grace but by "his *glorious* grace"—divine grace to match and over-match every reason you think God might give up on you and walk away. Whatever your family might face in the future, you can count on God to be gloriously gracious. That's who God is. And who God is matters more than who you are—even more than who you've been.

So go ahead. Dare to believe in God's grace. Believe in it defiantly, hopefully, expectantly. No matter what you've thought before about how far his grace can go and what his grace can do, his heart of mercy invites you to start believing this: *your family* can "walk in newness of life." Then, with that confidence, you can face every family heartache that needs his healing presence. You're not forced to stay stuck where you are. You can begin again—and again, and again—and never exhaust his goodness. Not today, and not in ten generations.

Two Steps Back to the Future

This chapter might be hard for you. We hope not. But there is no pain like family pain. Then again, there is no grace like God's grace. King David knew both experiences well. It's why he could say, "The LORD is near to the brokenhearted and saves the crushed in spirit" (Ps. 34:18).

But the blessing of God on people in pain is not a one-time download, so that we never need to come back for more. Our endless brokenness is met by his constant newness. So when sin has harmed a family, God has given us two linked pathways into his renewing grace.

1. Repentance

No one needs to fear repentance. After all, the goal is not a sinless family; the goal is an honest family. Who wouldn't want to live there? And it's the dad and mom who set that tone in the home, by being honest about their own sin. Pride fears and suppresses honesty: "Come on, why go overboard here? Your sin isn't *that* bad. And you don't want to look fanatical. What have you done that anybody else hasn't done?" But to these hypocritical thoughts we put our foot down and say, "No!" When we've sinned and injured our family, we owe them honest *repentance*. Then the air can start to clear. Besides, it's God's grace, kindness, and patience in the gospel, not anyone's yelling and screaming, that leads us to that repentance (Rom. 2:4).

Repentance is more than remorse. The theologian J. I. Packer put it plainly: "Repentance means starting to live a new life."[1] Picture a soldier marching in one direction, but then he stops, does a 180-degree about-face, and starts marching quick-time in the opposite direction. That's what repentance looks like. And the more consistently we keep marching in the gospel's new direction, the more healing we and our family can experience. We're still not perfect. Not by a long shot. We still need ongoing, midcourse corrections. But Martin Luther spoke truly in his Ninety-Five Theses: "When our Lord and Master Jesus Christ said, 'Repent,' he meant the entire life of believers to be one of repentance."[2]

Real repentance is not just momentary regret but a whole lifestyle adjustment. Think of that. Any family can make progress walking that path together. It's "newness of life" for imperfect people who want something better.

We all know what happens when we're *not* marching in the new gospel direction. We sweep wrongs under the rug. We minimize our sins by making excuses. We avoid embarrassing but needed conversations. We end up creating a family culture where everyone pretends with each other and walks around on eggshells, where everyone is expected to stifle their pain rather than face it and work through it together, by God's grace.

But true repentance means the offender owns up and makes things right again—as right as they can be made. Repentance means humbly admitting the horrible truth of our sin, with no excuses. Repentance means saying to our spouse and our children, "Now help me see myself," and then listening to what they tell us. And the sooner the better. Probably not when tensions are still running high. But at some point, the sin must be brought out into the open like this, where there's no place to hide. Humble honesty is where healing can begin. "God opposes the proud but gives grace to the humble" (1 Pet. 5:5). Avoidance only makes things worse.

Trust us on this: *If you will humble yourself under God's grace, you and your future will be defined not by your sins in the past but by your repentance in the present.* Your problems won't be solved quickly and easily. But when sin has been called sin, when the ugliness of it has been spoken and confessed, when the wrongs others have endured from it have been grieved over, when amends have been made—when it's obvious that repentance is taking over—then the family members can feel safe and even start trusting again. Maybe slowly, but surely. Together your family can begin to breathe the fresh air of hope in the gospel. The offender will feel relieved too. As a great man once said, "The more you deepen your repentance, the more room you have in your heart for the rivers of living water."[3] Wouldn't it be refreshing for those rivers to wash over you and everyone in your family?

Set a new tone of honesty in your family, starting with you. Change direction toward being "fully pleasing" to the Lord (Col. 1:10). Commit to "repent and turn to God, performing deeds in keeping with their repentance" (Acts 26:20). If you will, making repentance your lifestyle, your family will rejoice over you for generations to come. They might not always agree with you, but they will admire you the way one of C. S. Lewis's friends admired him as "the most thoroughly converted man I ever met."[4]

2. Forgiveness

Repentance is hard. Forgiveness is harder.

The section on repentance was for the one who's sinned. This section is for those who've been sinned against.

It isn't always obvious which is which. Family conflict can get complicated. Sometimes the person perceived as the "offender" in a family is the one who's trying to *obey* God. Sometimes, when following Christ, "a person's enemies will be those of his own household" (Matt. 10:36). This is a horrible experience. Sadly, it does happen.

But this section is about real sins needing real forgiveness. And if a lifestyle of honest repentance is key to your family's future, so is forgiveness. Deep, sincere, complete forgiveness of real sins. That's not easy, is it?

So we'll talk for a minute while you take a deep breath and get ready.

For starters, know this. If your family suffers or has suffered a catastrophic betrayal, it isn't the end of your tenth-generation blessing. In fact, it can be a new beginning, as together you believe in God's grace at a deeper level. The crisis is not the sin itself. The real crisis would be the despair that forgets God's grace and declares total war on the sinner.

And if it does go horribly wrong, and the whole tragic mess really does blow your family apart? Your story is still not over because God's grace is not over. For the rest of your life, you will be able to love other brokenhearted sufferers with an understanding and a tenderness that only the wounded deeply feel, and you will bring them hope. God is faithful, when everyone else fails. His blessing will flow through you more deeply than ever before, to the tenth generation of the spiritual family he will give you. And your spiritual family is the one you can keep forever.

> The crisis is not the sin itself. The real crisis would be the despair that forgets God's grace and declares total war on the sinner.

But for now, let's step back in here where repentance is crying out for forgiveness. How do you do it? If you are willing to forgive the family member who has wronged you, it will flow out at two levels—hidden deep in your heart and shown openly in the relationship.

First, *in your heart*: "Be kind to one another, tenderhearted, forgiving one another, as God in Christ forgave you" (Eph. 4:32). Deep within, God calls you to forgive this person freely and quickly, even before they repent. That's the tenderhearted forgiveness of Ephesians 4:32, getting everything out of your heart that might refuse to listen to his or her honest, brokenhearted repentance.

Second, *in the relationship*: "If your brother sins, rebuke him, and if he repents, forgive him" (Luke 17:3). This forgiveness is conditional: "*If* he repents, forgive him." The wise pastor John Stott explains:

> We are to rebuke a brother if he sins against us; we are to forgive him if he repents—and only if he repents. We must beware of cheapening forgiveness. . . . If a brother who has sinned against us refuses to repent, we should not forgive him. Does this startle you? It is what Jesus taught. . . . "Forgiveness" includes restoration to fellowship. If we can restore to full and intimate fellowship with ourselves a sinning and unrepentant brother, we reveal not the depth of our love but its shallowness, for we are doing what is not for his highest

good. A forgiveness which bypasses the need for repentance issues not from love but from sentimentality.[5]

Jesus describes your forgiveness-with-restoration in four steps:

Step 1: "If your brother sins. . . ." It's not about your own disappointed expectations. The worst part of any sin is that it's a sin against God. Jesus is saying, in essence, "If your family member behaves in a way that, according to Scripture, goes against God's will, then the first step is calling it sin."

Step 2: "If your brother sins, rebuke him." Since Jesus is the one speaking here, he cannot mean angry screaming. His kind of rebuke is calm. Maybe like this: "Dear one, in the Bible God says we should not do [blank]. But on that painful occasion, you did. You sinned. And your sin has injured our relationship. But I long for my trust in you and my respect for you to be restored. Please repent." No vague generalities, only concrete specifics, clearly addressed by the Bible.

It will help to avoid saying "You *are* . . ." That's too absolute, too global. The words "always" and "never" don't work either. Blasting the offender to smithereens leaves them with no place to stand where they can turn and repent. A wise rebuke limits itself to actual deeds done, actual words spoken, rather than the offender's motives or personality.

Step 3: "And if he repents. . . . " Jesus says "if" rather than "when," because pride can dig in. But if the offender humbly repents, healing can begin. How could it be otherwise? How can a sin be forgiven if it isn't confessed as sin? Hopefully the offender will say, after thinking it over, "You're right. I see it now. I *was* wrong. I'm sorry. And God helping me, this will never happen again. Now is there anything I can do to make it up to you?" This is what John the Baptist meant when he called all of us to "produce fruit consistent with repentance" (Luke 3:8 CSB).

But please keep this in mind. Your dear family member, now devastated, might not be able to undo all the damage done or re-create all the good destroyed. For example, how does a penitent sinner give back sleepless nights or an unabused body or lost innocence? Those are big questions. Those are fair questions. But it's at this point that the grace of God can flow through you in a new way. Here's how: Accept, deeply accept, that you will never recover everything this person's sin has cost you, and trust God to make it up to you in his own way. *He will.*

God is a redeemer of damaged lives. And the privilege your Redeemer is giving you as the victim is twofold. First, you can guide the offender toward ways they *can* make up for *some* of the harm done. Don't ask the impossible. But if the offender will do what they can, they themselves will be assured that their repentance is real. Second, you can imitate Christ by absorbing the remaining impact of the wrong rather than retaliating for it, even as Christ absorbed the full impact of your sins. He understands. He will walk with you and help you. And wherever you go in this brokenhearted world, you will bring his healing presence to wounded people with power that helps them and with beauty that adorns you.

Step 4: "And if he repents, forgive him." Now you are ready to bless your offender with the words you've longed to say: "Dear one, thank you for receiving my rebuke. I do forgive you—completely!" The Lord has blessed your family with the peace, the healing *shalom*, you were praying for. Now your future together has a chance. Walk forward—gently, wisely, in "newness of life" (Rom. 6:4).

Corrie ten Boom and her sister Betsie suffered in a Nazi concentration camp during World War II. After the war, Corrie spoke at a Christian gathering in Germany. Her topic was forgiveness, and her message was simple:

> When we confess our sins, God casts them into the deepest ocean, gone forever. And even though I cannot find a Scripture for it, I believe God then places a sign out there that says, NO FISHING ALLOWED.[6]

As the event concluded, a man slowly approached her out of the crowd. Suddenly Corrie remembered him. He had been one of the most sadistic guards in that horrible camp. But he'd repented of his atrocities and become a believer in Christ. He stood there, his hand stretched out in an appeal, asking Corrie, "Fraulein, will you forgive me?" She explains what happened next:

> I stood there—I whose sins had again and again to be forgiven—and could not forgive. Betsie had died in that place—could he erase her slow terrible death simply for the asking?
>
> It could not have been many seconds that he stood there—hand held out—but to me it seemed hours as I wrestled with the most difficult thing I had ever had to do. . . .
>
> And still I stood there with the coldness clutching my heart. But forgiveness is not an emotion—I knew that too. Forgiveness is an act of the will, and the will can function regardless of the temperature of the heart. "Jesus, help me!" I prayed silently. "I can lift my hand. I can do that much. You supply the feeling."
>
> And so woodenly, mechanically, I thrust my hand into the one stretched out to me. And as I did, an incredible thing took place. The current started in my shoulder, raced down my arm, sprang into our joined hands. And then this healing warmth seemed to flood my whole being, bringing tears to my eyes.

"I forgive you, brother!" I cried. "With all my heart."

For a long moment we grasped each other's hands, the former guard and the former prisoner. I had never known God's love so intensely as I did then.

"With all my heart." The impossible becomes possible. The anger we've kept locked inside, as if its presence protected us from being hurt so badly again—we let it go. It's like a shard of broken glass being pulled from our body—painful at first, but then—*relief!* It's out. It wasn't helping us. It was hurting us. It was killing us. Now it's gone. And suddenly, the trajectory of your family is free from this heavy weight you've been dragging around. The future you share between you, the future of your whole family, can now move from denial to honesty and hope.

Grace is this whole new, beautiful way of navigating family life.

In *The Lion, The Witch and the Wardrobe*, C. S. Lewis paints the picture of the moment your family might need right now. Edmund has behaved selfishly. His sin has cost Peter and Lucy and Susan heavily. It would cost Aslan (the Jesus figure in the story) his very life. But the Lion has a talk with Edmund, and it changes the boy. Then Aslan brings him back to his family:

> "Here is your brother," he said, "and—there
> is no need to talk to him about what is past."

Edmund shook hands with each of the others and said to each of them in turn, "I'm sorry," and everyone said, "That's all right."[7]

Your family can be living proof of God's "for no reason" grace. The Bible says, "All this is from God, who through Christ reconciled us to himself and gave us the ministry of reconciliation" (2 Cor. 5:18). It isn't about *moments* of reconciliation now and then, when we feel like it, but the *ministry* of reconciliation all the time. Why not let this glorious, costly, healing vision into your heart? You and your family can say together, "Reconciliation—it's just how we roll now. We're a gospel family!"

Jesus told a story about a man who didn't see things this way, who refused to forgive a person that owed him a debt, even though the man himself had just been forgiven a much larger debt (Matt. 18:21–35). The point was clear: "Should not you have had mercy on your fellow servant, as I had mercy on you?" (v. 33).

Having spent time in this passage recently, we were deeply moved—so much so, that Ray turned his thoughts into a prayer.[8] Maybe you'd like to join us in praying it:

> O Lord of grace abounding, even to me,
> you whose heart delights to show mercy where
> severity would be appropriate, and grace where
> justice could rightly punish, so touch my

broken heart with your healing heart, that I become *the most forgiving, reconciling, relaxed, peaceable person I'll ever meet in all this world,* with a heart that cheerfully "loves much" (Luke 7:47), to the praise of your glorious grace. Through Christ and his merits I pray. Amen.

Why not live a little dangerously? Why not give your heart away, all over again, to your broken family? Why not become, by God's grace, the most forgiving, reconciling, relaxed, peaceable family member you will ever meet? The future will long feel the impact of your healing presence. How could it not be so? God's grace is the most enduring power in all this world.

CHAPTER 9

Your Surprising Path Forward

"His mercy is for those who fear him
from generation to generation."
Luke 1:50

uke 1:50 comes from the lips of Mary, the mother of Jesus. God's mercy had reached out to her, even to her, a little nobody from Nowheresville in the boondocks of the Roman Empire. Let *that* sink in. The all-holy God above, who'd promised ages before to build a whole new world, shunned Caesar and his world-dominating powers. Instead, he drew near to Mary with his world-redeeming mercies.

What thrilled her was God's surprising way of creating his better world—snubbing the heavy hitters and sending his Son as a humble man, through a humble woman. (Read it for yourself sometime soon—Luke 1:46–55.) God just loves lifting up the lowly, to defeat the mighty. Mary was living proof of it, and it changed how she saw herself and her family and the future.

And if you fear the Lord, you too are proving how God redirects history toward the redeeming display of his glory. That's the whole point of Luke 1:50—the long-standing ways of God, from Genesis to Revelation, building a new world that will last forever. The people he uses are the humble, the unimpressive, the weak. How does it work? We bring our need, and he gives his mercy. Then we bring more need, and he gives more mercy—"pardoning mercy, healing mercy, accepting mercy, crowning mercy," to quote a scholar from centuries ago.[1] It's God's standard *modus operandi*. It's how, in a way we don't understand, something profound happens. His purpose of grace starts small, opens wide, and reaches far, more and more. Watch in wonder: "His mercy is for those who fear him"—for how long?—"from generation to generation" (Luke 1:50). There is no expiration date on that assurance.

That's why Mary rejoiced—maybe with tears of wonder on her cheeks. She felt included. She felt significant. She knew she mattered in something God was doing that he'd started long before her and would still be doing long after she was gone. Jesus the Messiah was coming—finally—and he was coming to stay. And thanks to him, Mary's little life and her soon-to-be family had become (what were the words we said about you at the beginning of this book?) *historically significant.*

"His mercy is for those who fear him from generation to generation." His new world welcomes you and your family, like it welcomed hers, to a future of unimaginable grandeur.

We're so excited, aren't you?

There's just nothing like being a gospel family. Believing the gospel. Embodying the gospel. Cherishing the staggering hope that makes the gospel so grand we can't quite catch our breath when we truly think about it. It's not up to you to make sure everything turns out perfectly for your family. You can't control that. But you can stand here, like Mary, like other believers throughout history, who stood gazing up at the mystery and majesty of God and his powerful, merciful love for this world and his people, and marvel that he has included us, even us, in it. *This* you can do. And your simple faith will matter from your generation to the next to the next to the next.

You can humbly fear the Lord.

Let's do that. It's how, God says, he showers his mercy upon us for ages and ages down the time line. Just humble reverence. Just that.

Does God's strategy for your future family feel like a letdown? Maybe. But an unimpressive strategy can work really well for unimpressive people. The surprising truth is, the low place is where we experience God. Down there is where you can begin your new journey, your path forward into your family's long-term blessing.

What Is the "Fear of the Lord"?

Let's go back to another character from Scripture. Abraham's family story shows us what it means to "fear the Lord" and the difference that makes.

After the human race spiraled down into self-destruction (Gen. 3–11), the Lord promised Abraham he would redeem this train-wreck of a world (Gen. 12–21). He said Abraham would have a son as the next step in the divine plan of world-rescue. But Abraham was old. His wife Sarah was old. God had timed it that way on purpose, so that the story would prove his miracle-working power was the secret, not only to *their* future but to ours. No surprise then, Abraham and Sarah did have a son, the miracle boy Isaac. His name means "laughter," because it was all so hilariously joyous that Isaac even came to exist. A great start to the best story in human history!

But then, it looked like disaster struck.

The Bible says "God tested Abraham" (Gen. 22:1). How? God said to him, in so many words, "Take your son Isaac, the joy of your heart, the key to your future and to the coming Savior of the world—take this precious boy and offer him to me as a sacrifice."

God's command shocked Abraham. It shocks us. But sooner or later, God tests every one of us. He throws our lives into bewildering upheaval. The life we expected implodes, leaving us with circumstances we can't explain and devastation we can barely endure. We don't go looking for these tests. They come and find us. And they always seem to make no sense. Yet inevitably, God will tell every one of us to let go even of his good gifts so that he himself, God alone, can tell our story in his own surprising way. And when he does, we watch his strategy turn out to be better than the straight, obvious, easy path we preferred.

Abraham passed the test with flying colors. He knew, way down deep, that God never breaks his promises. He didn't know what was happening or why this was being asked of him, yet he believed that, even if Isaac died, the Lord would raise him from the dead (Heb. 11:17–19). Yes, it must have hurt Abraham deeply to lay his son Isaac on that altar. But he humbly obeyed God, moment by moment. That's what fearing the Lord looks like.

In fact, the only thing Abraham said to God throughout the ordeal was "Here am I" (Gen. 22:1, 11). That was Abraham's whole response to God. Just three words: "Here am I." What Abraham meant was, "Lord, you promised me this son. Now you're taking him away. But I believe you'll give him back to me because you always keep your promises. So this is your story to tell, not mine. Here am I, whatever you want."

How did God respond to Abraham's reverent fear? He stopped Abraham from sacrificing Isaac. Then he said, "Now I know that you fear God, seeing you have not withheld your son, your only son, from me" (v. 12).

Mary herself said to God at the surprising, disruptive news of the birth of her son Jesus, "Behold, I am the servant of the Lord; let it be to me according to your word" (Luke 1:38). She was saying, like Abraham, "Here am I." She too kept saying yes to God's plan, moment by moment.

So now we know:

> Fearing the Lord means we let him tell our
> story, saying yes to him moment by moment.

It means we put him first when everything is on the line. It means we follow him when it costs us. It means we trust his promises when our lives appear to deny his promises. It means we do the right thing even when no one but God is looking. It means we are not only available to him but also expendable for him.

> The fear of the Lord is when we let real Christianity, not our preferences, define our path forward.

In other words, the fear of the Lord is when we let real Christianity, not our preferences, define our path forward. *Why* would we do such a thing? Because "his mercy is for those who fear him from generation to generation." It's what the Bible says.

Your family, to the tenth generation, needs this powerful, hopeful legacy from you. And not much else. Thankfully they can see it in you during the good times, when they recognize how you thank God for every moment of simple happiness together as a family—a Monopoly game on the living room floor, fishing at the lake on summer vacation, cheering at the Little League game, good grades from school, and all the joys of family life. But you show your family something greater by walking in the fear of the Lord even when it's hard, even when you suffer, especially when you suffer, because they will suffer too.

In *The Screwtape Letters*, a fascinating book by C. S. Lewis that turns Christianity on its head by seeing it from the devil's point of view, a mentor demon is coaching a trainee demon, which means the "Enemy" in this quote is God:

> Do not be deceived, Wormwood. Our cause is never more in danger than when a human, no longer desiring, but still intending, to do our Enemy's will, looks round upon a universe from which every trace of Him seems to have vanished, and asks why he has been forsaken, and still obeys.[2]

Your steady, faithful integrity—*this* is the fear of the Lord your future family needs from you. "His mercy is for those who fear him"—who fear him like that!—"from generation to generation." Not because we ever *deserve* his mercy. We never do. But we *believe* in his mercy, so we follow him, step by step, no matter what.

Great things happen when we start treating God as God. He makes sure our reverent humility trends well: "The reward for humility and the fear of the LORD is riches and honor and life" (Prov. 22:4). And in the moments when it's hard to walk this path, we keep going, by sheer faith. And in keeping on and keeping on and keeping on, we keep blessing our future family. Nominal Christianity would be a curse to our children. But a real, rugged faith in Christ is a blessing to our children. They're sure going to need it in their time. And our time to show it to them is *now*, whatever test we're facing.

Maybe your next step, for your children's sake, is to become a child yourself, as you stand before your Father God. Jesus said, "Truly I say to you, whoever does not receive the kingdom of God like a child shall not enter it" (Mark 10:15). The kingdom of God is the new world you long for your family to live in forever. But have you humbled yourself like a child? Have you welcomed King Jesus into your life, with no preconditions, no limits? If so, then you do fear the Lord. Your life is wonderfully marked by "that affectionate reverence by which the child of God bends himself humbly and carefully to his Father's law."[3] Your future is looking good, and you are already blessing your family out there in that future.

Remember what God said to Abraham? "Because you have done this and have not withheld your son, your only son, I will surely bless you" (Gen. 22:16–17). That promise trickled down through history, all the way to Jesus—the Son who was *not* spared but *was* sacrificed—so that we would forever be spared. That's the gospel. That's the confidence of a gospel-centered person. Why not let it set the tone of your family? Fearing the Lord is the only hopeful path forward for anyone, from generation to generation. It outlasts this whole world.

What Can We Expect from Mercy?

When Mary said God's mercy is "for those who fear him from generation to generation," she was probably thinking of a famous passage she knew from Old Testament Scripture: "The steadfast love of the LORD is from everlasting to everlasting on those who fear him, and his righteousness to children's children" (Ps. 103:17). God doesn't change over time.[4] The God we read about in the Bible is the same God who is here with you right now, even as you read this page. And this God, with all his mighty heart, is *merciful*. His mercy is the theme of the whole Bible.

Here is your assurance: This merciful God will still be there two hundred years from now, when your family is in their tenth generation, with all their needs.

Look at this One we can count on *always*. The Bible says he is "rich in mercy" (Eph. 2:4)—not budgeting his mercies but "rich" in them. And he is a *big* spender. The Bible says he is "abounding in mercy" (Exod. 34:6 Berkeley). His mercies are like ocean swells rising into mighty waves that we don't cause but we sure can surf. The Bible speaks of God's "great mercy" (1 Pet. 1:3) and his "tender mercy" (Luke 1:78). His mercy is both massive and emotional, both generous and heartfelt. His mercy for us isn't a 51/49 calculation, on a good day, as if things could go either way. He isn't hemming and hawing: "Will I bring the hammer down on this ridiculous sinner who should know better by now, or will I be merciful?" His *great* heart is *tenderly* merciful. This is who God *is*. It's why one scholar describes the God of the Bible as "kind and sensitive."[5]

> His mercies are like ocean swells rising into mighty waves that we don't cause but we sure can surf.

So, again, now we know:

God is why God sticks with us long-term.

We don't keep him motivated; he keeps our hearts open. And he is all-in all the time.

Our merciful God.

When we read the Bible, we sometimes wonder how it applies today. The dramatic miracles, for example—Jesus healing lepers—is he still doing that today? It's okay to debate the question. But *the whole point* of the biblical phrase, "his mercy is for those who fear him from generation to generation," is the unchanging, permanent, rock-solid certainty of God's mercy, for as long as we're going to need him.

You worry about your family's future, of course. You care deeply. So do we. But here is our go-to verse in all our moments of fear:

> "His mercy is for those who fear him from generation to generation."

Announce this verse to yourself, as often as you need to. Martin Luther was laughably blunt about it. He said the good news of God's mercy "cannot be beaten into our ears enough or too much."[6] Bad news feels natural to us; the good news is an adjustment. You'll never drift your way into hope. You must be decisive. You can get there, and you stay there, by renouncing your dark thoughts of God and daring to believe the promised mercies of God.

God's mercy, then, is his heartfelt care for the undeserving. We bring nothing to him but our failures and needs. We hold out before him the empty hands of faith. And to our amazement, we discover over and over again that God loves to pour out his mercies for the undeserving! He loves it so much that he's promised to keep doing it for a long, long time.

Luke 1:50 is a mighty weapon for your fight.

Use it.

Don't be afraid.

Fear only God.

And trust his mercy.
From now on.
And on and on.

A Prayer for Your Family's Long-Term Blessing

Maybe your mind is racing with new ideas for investing in your family's future. Wonderful! Don't lose those ideas. Jot them down. Get excited about it. It's going to be hard sometimes, but it's going to be fun too.

In fact, how'd you like to give the devil a really bad day—and have fun doing it? After all, he shoves his despair down your throat all the time. Why not get even by defiantly rejoicing, for your own soul's sake, and for your future family's sake, in the wonderful mercies God has planned for you and for them? Staking all your hope on God alone, throw your head back and laugh the laugh of faith, confident that you have won big-time. *God* is for you, and he is for your family. In fact, he is already out ahead of you, present and involved in that future you are tempted to fear!

Just make sure of this. Stay low before the Lord. Everything hopeful comes down from above and lands in that low place of fearing him. Stay humble. Stay open. And teach your children both his mercy and your reverence. Is there any greater legacy you could leave?

Here at the end of our journey together, we hope this moment will be a new beginning for you and for your family, from generation to generation. The fresh start you desire, the new energy and resolve and purpose and direction and sacrifice, with new spring in your step, new sparkle in your eye, new steel in your spine—that's what we're praying for you. That's what we're praying for ourselves too.

Why don't we just stop right here and pray together?

An old prayer from John Wesley (1703–1791) puts into words the reverence that God loves to bless. *You* can pray this prayer of Wesley's. And teach your family to pray it. If you don't like reading your prayers, pray something like it in your own words.

This old prayer is serious, even scary. But it's just basic Christianity. And it is freeing, it is powerful—a creative force that will keep your feet on the path of blessing. God will not fail to answer your prayer, thanks to Jesus and his cross. Thanks to the gospel. But settling for less than total openness to the Lord—let's be honest, that would be playing games with God. Why should he honor that? Why should our children respect that?

Here's what we're asking you to do. *Join us in making this prayer a defining presence in your family for the rest of your life.* Pray it together. Discuss it together. Have this prayer done up in calligraphy, sign it, date it, frame it, hang it in a prominent place in your home. Plant your flag here. Let this prayer wash over your precious family, on into the future. And you will see God answer this prayer, for his glory, with many mercies.

Here then is Wesley's prayer,[7] adapted for your family:

> O God, our Savior,
> We are no longer our own but yours.
> Put us to what you will.
> Rank us with whom you will.
> Put us to doing, put us to suffering.
> Let us be employed for you or laid aside for
>   you,
> exalted for you or brought low for you.
> Let us be full, let us be empty.
> Let us have all things, let us have nothing.
> We freely and wholeheartedly yield all things
> to your pleasure and disposal.
> And now, O glorious and blessed God,
> Father, Son and Holy Spirit,
> you are ours, and we are yours.
> So be it.
> And the covenant we have made on earth,
> let it be ratified in heaven.
> Amen.

Ten Truths to the Tenth Generation

"I will pour water on the thirsty land,
and streams on the dry ground; I will
pour my Spirit upon your offspring, and
my blessing on your descendants."
Isaiah 44:3

We're hesitant to let you go, but we know you've got a life to lead—and now, ten generations to go get ready for! But before we say our goodbyes and head off with new purpose for the next new day, here are ten brief statements to sum up the time we've spent together. Ten biblical insights into the ways of God with your family, far into the future.

1. The wraparound assurance for your family is *covenant.*

She is your companion and your wife by covenant. (Mal. 2:14)

The Bible opens our eyes to beauty this world never would have shown us. Modern culture trivializes relationships as mere human arrangements, easily reshaped according to our preferences. With husbands and wives, with parents and children, we're told there is no God-given pattern to follow. We're left with our mere desires to satisfy, while our kaleidoscopic impulses change from one moment to the next. No wonder many homes are in turmoil.

The Bible shows us a better way. Here is the key insight: *our God is a covenant-making, covenant-keeping God.* He makes promises, then he keeps them. (Imagine that.) He obligates himself, then he follows through.[1] And since he created us in his image, we flourish not by following our crazy desires but by living in covenant faithfulness.

Marriage is a prime example: ". . . your wife *by covenant*," the Bible says. Marriage is a sacred covenant we enter into through our wedding vows. Yes, there are personal aspects of our marriages that we improvise. But marriage itself is predefined by God and, wonderfully, preapproved by God. Marriage comes from God to us as a blessing we enjoy, not a blank we fill in. Marriage dignifies us with lasting obligations and cheers us with joyous expectations. It's not so much a script to follow but more a dance to learn, with steps and moves that display the beauty God had in mind for us.

Here's the point. Marriage *as a covenant* enhances family stability. It nurtures cooperation. And it sets a tone of grown-up, calm confidence in a home, where children can feel safe and happy. So always remember, *your marriage was designed by God.* If you will honor him for revealing it, he will honor you for receiving it. And his blessing will carry over into your future family.

2. God's blessing moves from one faithful generation to the next.

"By myself I have sworn, declares the LORD, because you have done this and have not withheld your son, your only son, I will surely bless you, and I will surely multiply your offspring as the stars of heaven and as the sand that is on the seashore. And your offspring shall possess the gate of his enemies, and in your offspring shall all the nations of the earth be blessed, because you have obeyed my voice." (Gen. 22:16–18)

The promises of God do not work automatically, like a factory churning out products on an assembly line. God is not a machine. We are not machines. He is our Father, and we are his family. The way he has chosen for his loving promises to get traction in our homes is by stirring up our *faith*. That's how we open up to him more and more. That's how his blessing moves forward into the future generations of your family.

You don't have to deserve him, but you do have to revere him. *The grace of God excludes your earning, but it doesn't exclude your effort.* His grace inspires your decisive, joyous, all-in devotion to the lordship of Jesus so that you put him first in your family. And then he blesses you for what he himself has inspired. Amazing grace!

What did God say about Abraham? "I have chosen him, that he may command his children and his household after him to keep the way of the LORD by doing righteousness and justice, so that the LORD may bring Abraham what he has promised him" (Gen. 18:19). Talk about "grace upon grace" (John 1:16)! The Bible puts it simply: "*by faith* Abraham obeyed" (Heb. 11:8, emphasis added).

If you will trust the Lord in this courageous way as you raise your children, they will be saying many years from now, "A big part of the blessing in our lives today is the way our parents followed Jesus back in their day. Thank you, Lord!"

TEN TRUTHS TO THE TENTH GENERATION

3. One reason God allows suffering: so your kids can see how real Jesus is.

> You shall tell your son on that day, "It is because of what the LORD did for me when I came out of Egypt." (Exod. 13:8)

A well-told story gets us sitting on the edge of our seats, wondering, "How are those poor people ever going to get out of *that* mess?!?" C. S. Lewis explained, it's how a good story works: "Dangers, of course, there must be; how else can you keep a story going?"[2] The Bible tells us that kind of story—for example, the liberation of God's family from horrible slavery in Egypt. That's the backstory to Exodus 13:8—"what the LORD did for [them]." And the memory of their surprising escape lasted long. Parents passed down to their children how God came through for them.

That's one reason God allows us parents to face insurmountable challenges today. *It is for our children's sake.* God himself is giving your family true stories to tell about his rescues, when everything was on the line. Then your children, steeped in the family adventure, will be strengthened for the unimaginable pressures they will surely face in their own time.

He even gives prodigals his stories to tell. We parents naturally worry that our children might drift from the Lord. After all, many of us, especially during our teen and young adult years, put some distance between ourselves and our parents' faith. But eventually, by God's grace, we had a change of heart. We stumbled home, like the prodigal son, and our heavenly Father received us not with a scolding but with an embrace. His grace changed us. We started loving the Lord, and we started respecting our parents' love for him. Without even intending to, we stepped into the generational linkage of biblical faith: "This is my God, and I will praise him, my father's God, and I will exalt him" (Exod. 15:2).

Yes, crazy prodigals make beautiful saints. And if God didn't give up on *us,* let's never give up on our wayward children. They might end up better Christians than we are—with even greater stories to tell of how real Jesus is.

4. One reason God gave you children: to keep *your* heart focused.

"Only take care, and keep your soul diligently, lest you forget the things that your eyes have seen, and lest they depart from your heart all the days of your life. Make them known to your children and your children's children— how on the day that you stood before the LORD your God at Horeb, the LORD said to me, 'Gather the people to me, that I may let them hear my words, so that they may learn to

fear me all the days that they live on the earth,
and that they may teach their children so.'"
(Deut. 4:9–10)

We forget yesterday's blessings as soon as today's pressures get up in our faces. But one way we parents can stay Jesus-aware every day is to keep up an ongoing conversation with our children—like over dinner, for example, at the end of the day. It can be as simple as this: "So, y'all, how did we experience God's blessing today?" Then with gentle wisdom, at an age-appropriate level, you help each child around the table share briefly in his or her own way. And you close the conversation with a brief prayer of thanks. No big production. Just simple, honest, real. Exactly what your children need from you. But this kind of family sharing does something for you too: it keeps *your* soul tender, day by day. You'll find yourself more aware of him as you help your family stay in that zone too.

Always remember, the greatest gift you can give to your children is your own sensitivity to the Lord.

5. God visits ordinary moments with his extraordinary presence.

"Hear, O Israel: The LORD our God, the LORD is one. You shall love the LORD your God with all your heart and with all your soul and

with all your might. And these words that I
command you today shall be on your heart.
You shall teach them diligently to your children, and shall talk of them when you sit in
your house, and when you walk by the way,
and when you lie down, and when you rise."
(Deut. 6:4–7)

Our children do not automatically navigate reality with a
wholehearted focus on God. Neither do we, right? But he graciously takes it easy on us. He locates his presence right where
every family can find him: in ordinary daily life. Here's one
way you can make this practical. Choose one verse of Scripture
for your family to talk about together each week: "The Jones
Family Verse of the Week!" Write it out on a big piece of tag-
board with a felt pen, including the chapter-and-verse reference. Hold it up at the breakfast table each morning and say
the verse and the reference out loud together. Naturally, it will
come up in other conversations too. But that's fifty-two verses
of Scripture a year, and 520 verses in a decade! And as you
know when you're raising children, a decade *flies* by.

Your family can discover, in the simplicity of ordinary life,
what it can look like to love the Lord Jesus with a whole heart,
refreshed again and again with the good news of the gospel.
And your children will *never* forget how much the Lord and
his Word meant to you.

6. Jesus is not a lifestyle enhancement. He is your family's very *life*.

"I have set before you life and death, blessing and curse. Therefore choose life, that you and your offspring may live, loving the LORD your God, obeying his voice and holding fast to him, for he is your life . . ." (Deut. 30:19–20)

When Jesus says, "Follow me" (Matt. 9:9), he is echoing this "choose life" command from the Old Testament. He sure isn't yelling at us, "Do better, try harder, pedal faster!" He is offering us the precious gift of *himself*. With him, we can calm down, breathe, rest. And who of us isn't fed up with this frantic world, not to mention our own embarrassing regrets? But that's why—*we* are why—Jesus says, "So, follow *me* for a change?" All he wants is to help us choose life, help us come alive, more and more. But we do have to choose. We must turn from our failed dreams and put our feet daily on his path of life. It's as simple as this. We say, "Okay, Lord. I'm a mess. But I'm *your* mess now." That's when great things start happening, "that you *and your offspring* may live."

When children grow up with a parent who is *alive* in Jesus, it's a lot easier for them to come alive too.

7. As your children are nurtured in the grace of Jesus, they will *flourish*.

May our sons in their youth be like plants full grown, our daughters like corner pillars cut for the structure of a palace. (Ps. 144:12)

There is nothing second-rate in Jesus. Yes, religion *without him* is misery. But as you set the tone of your family with the life-enriching grace of Christ, they will feel it.

Attracted by your freedom of spirit, your sons, following the Lord, can flourish "like plants full grown"—deeply rooted below, with nothing between them and heaven above. Your daughters, following the Lord, can stand strong and tall "like corner pillars cut for the structure of a palace"—think of the Caryatids at the Acropolis in Athens.

Here then is something you *must* say to your children: "I honestly don't care if you get into a prestigious university, land a high-paying job, and become a 'big deal' in this world. But I beg this of you—that you will love Jesus and live for him, whatever that looks like for you!" Yes, your kids might roll their eyes—at the moment. But soon enough, this seductive world will break their hearts. Then they will remember what you said. And your words will open a door for them to come back to Jesus and discover how good he really is. That's when your children will not just heal but will also start to flourish.

8. Our sins harm our families, but God is able to rebuild what we damage.

Do good to Zion in your good pleasure; build
up the walls of Jerusalem. (Ps. 51:18)

Let's face ourselves and our sins honestly. Repentance is
always a "next step" for us sinners, again and again. But what
about our sins that have harmed our families? What about the
opportunities we've lost, the trust we've betrayed, the cruelties
we've shouted, the love we've withheld? Every parent has regrets.

That's why Psalm 51 is in the Bible. It invites us into
repentance *and restoration*. In verse 18, David faced into the
damage his sins had done to others. What he tore down by
his own selfishness, he asked God to rebuild in his good pleasure. Maybe Psalm 51 is perfect for you right now. If your sins
have damaged your family's faith in you, and even their faith in
God, he is ready to help you rebuild. It won't be easy. But the
Lord will be with you.

It starts with honest prayer, like Psalm 51:18. You might
translate it like this: "Lord, I have wronged my family. I
repent—deeply. I ask you now to do good to my family in your
good pleasure. I ask you to rebuild the walls of safety, protection, and trust my recklessness has torn down. It's my fault,
Lord. But now I am asking you to rebuild my heart and my
family, by your grace, for your glory."

God *loves* to hear and answer our brokenhearted prayers.

9. Your investment in your family can continue long after you die.

The righteous who walks in his integrity—
blessed are his children after him! (Prov. 20:7)

If "the memory of the righteous is a blessing" (Prov. 10:7), and it sure is, then you can be a blessing to your family for a long, long time. How? It starts right now, right here: *Give yourself to Christ.* Hand yourself clear over to him. And tell him so, out loud, maybe on your knees. Then take it one step at a time, upheld by his gracious hand, all the way to the end. Even as your body ages, your soul will sweeten and grow richer and fuller, overflowing with hope for your family around you:

> The righteous flourish like the palm tree
> and grow like a cedar in Lebanon. They are
> planted in the house of the LORD; they flour-
> ish in the courts of our God. They still bear
> fruit in old age; they are ever full of sap and
> green. (Ps. 92:12–14)

Then long after you die, you will remain very present with your family as an inspiring memory. They will think of you. They will speak of you. They will say things like, "Remember how Dad kept trusting Jesus through his cancer? Remember how Mom walked with the Lord through her heartbreak at Dad's death? God's grace was mightily upon them—all the way!" And your family will draw strength from you. Then they, in their turn, will live well, and they will die well.

One generation will keep on blessing another, even to the tenth.

10. Your final hope for your children is not your amazing parenting but God's amazing grace.

> O LORD, the God of Abraham, Isaac and Israel, our fathers, keep forever such purposes and thoughts in the hearts of your people, and direct their hearts toward you. (1 Chron. 29:18)

Having done all you can and should do for your children, grandchildren, and beyond, how do you conclude? Where do you rest? *You bow low before the God of all grace, and you put all your hope in him alone.* Only he can keep holy purposes in the hearts of your family. Only he can direct their hearts toward Christ. And he can. He really can. That's why this verse is in the Bible—to give you hope beyond your shortcomings, certainly beyond your best efforts. The God of all grace is able to keep a "hedge" of protection around your family (Job 1:10), delivering them from evil and keeping them close to himself.

Thanks to the merit of Christ, you have every right to pray boldly, "O Lord God, set my dear family apart to yourself, to the tenth generation. *Your kingdom come, your will be done, through this family.* Why else do we even exist? For this I pray. To this I dedicate myself. In the holy name of Christ, and for his sake. Amen!"

Acknowledgments

We thank our dear children—Eric, Krista, Dane, and Gavin—for contributing to our book. We are honored by their presence.

We thank our two oldest grandchildren, Kate and Zach, for sharing their highlights from Our Family Gathering in July 2023.

We thank our assistant, Gena Mayse, for her faithful support while we devoted ourselves to this task.

We are thankful for Ray's dad, Ray Ortlund Sr. We feel privileged to include excerpts from his outstanding sermon, "Claim Your Children for Christ," preached in 1976.

We thank our precious friends on the Board of Renewal Ministries—David and Ashley Edwards, Byron and Anne Morris, John and Melinda Perry, Howard and Dawn Varnedoe—for their guidance and prayers through the years.

We thank our editor and friend, Lawrence Kimbrough, for helping us refine and polish our writing.

We thank our agents, Austin Wilson and Andrew Wolgemuth, for advising and supporting us along the way.

We thank all our friends at B&H Publishing for their personal kindness and professional expertise.

We thank God for the privilege of life, family, and purpose worthy of our all.

Recommended Resources

William J. Bennett, *The Children's Book of Virtues* (Simon & Schuster, 1995).

> In a world of corruption, here is an inspiring resource for helping your children see and embrace what is good and right and humane.

https://canopy.us/

> An essential safeguard: user-friendly computer software for protecting your family from toxic online content.

Captains Courageous, starring Spencer Tracy, Lionel Barrymore, and Freddie Bartholomew (MGM, 1937).

> This classic movie tells the story of a boy growing up to be a man, and a father discovering what it means to be a dad.

Andy Crouch, *The Tech-Wise Family: Everyday Steps for Putting Technology in its Proper Place* (Baker, 2017).

> Doable strategies for overcoming the new hurdle to healthy family life: the intrusive presence of electronic devices that diminish the human warmth every family needs.

Elisabeth Elliot, *Let Me Be a Woman* (Tyndale, 1999).

> An articulate invitation into God's plan for the glories of true womanhood, written by a wise and profound Christian woman.

It's a Wonderful Life, starring James Stewart and Donna Reed (Liberty Films, 1946).

> Your life is so worth living, even when you feel like a failure. George Bailey's story helps us keep going and even rejoice in the face of challenges—by faith in God.

C. S. Lewis, *The Lion, the Witch and the Wardrobe* (HarperCollins, 2000).

> The classic read-aloud story of children who fall into danger—only to discover the grace and glory of Jesus, the true King.

Sally Lloyd-Jones, *The Jesus Storybook Bible* (ZonderKidz, 2007).

> Your children can learn to read the Bible with gospel eyes, so that they grow strong with confidence in the grace of Christ.

Jani Ortlund, *A Child's First Book about Marriage* (Christian Focus, 2018).

> We live in an age of such confusion that we parents must teach our children what marriage really is. If we don't teach them, the world will mis-teach them.

Jani Ortlund, *His Loving Law, Our Lasting Legacy: Living the Ten Commandments and Giving Them to our Children* (Crossway, 2007).

> A guide for raising your children in the practical integrity that honors God and strengthens a family for long-term faithfulness.

Ray Ortlund, *Marriage and the Mystery of the Gospel* (Crossway, 2016).

> Your marriage is more than your marriage. It is also a prophetic statement from God himself that his love for you is permanent—and even romantic. Who knew?

J. I. Packer, *Praying the Lord's Prayer* (Crossway, 2007).

> The key to your family's future is not you achieving complete control but you turning to God in prayer, and the best way to pray is how our Lord himself taught us.

Edith Schaeffer, *What Is a Family?* (Baker, 1997).

> An inspiring, uplifting vision of the human beauty your family is and can become—more and more.

Francis Schaeffer, *The Lord's Work in the Lord's Way and No Little People* (Crossway, 2022).

> This world makes all of us feel small. But there are no little people, not in the sight of God. You matter! Your family matters!

Paul Tournier, *To Understand Each Other: Classic Wisdom on Marriage* (John Knox, 1969).

> Deep and practical insights into how your marriage can be a continuous discovery of both yourself and your mate.

Jim Trelease, *The Read-Aloud Handbook* (Penguin, 2019).

> A treasure-trove of resources and encouragements for reading aloud to your children, giving them a "taste" for reading from their early years.

Notes

Chapter 1

1. John G. Paton, *John G. Paton, Missionary to the New Hebrides: An Autobiography* (New York: Fleming H. Revell, 1889), 40–42.

Chapter 2

1. G. K. Beale, *Redemptive Reversals and the Ironic Overturning of Human Wisdom* (Wheaton, IL: Crossway, 2019), 184: "True believers are like their representative Jesus Christ. The restorative irony displayed in Christ's suffering life and death is also displayed in their lives because they are being conformed to Christ's image (Rom. 8:29); that is, they live a cruciform life whereby their faith in the midst of their suffering indicates that they are winning spiritual victory in the midst of their seeming defeat. Such faith indicates that they are actually spiritually strong and on the road to ultimate victory, both spiritually and physically, in the new heavens and the new earth."

2. Henry Barclay Swete, *The Gospel According to St. Mark* (London: Macmillan and Co., 1927), 222. A. T. Robertson, *Word Pictures in the New Testament* (Nashville: Broadman Press, 1930), I:351: "Jesus repeatedly blessed them, laying his hands upon each of them. It was a great moment for each mother and child."

3. Quoted in Timothy George, *Theology of the Reformers* (Nashville: Broadman Press, 1988), 323.

Chapter 3

1. See Ray Ortlund, *Marriage and the Mystery of the Gospel* (Wheaton: Crossway, 2016), 79–103.

2. We thank our friend John Piper for that wording: John Piper, *This Momentary Marriage: A Parable of Permanence* (Wheaton: Crossway, 2012).

3. Alastair Roberts, quoted in Graham Beynon and Jane Tooher, *Embracing Complementarianism: Turning Biblical Convictions into Positive Church Culture* (Epsom: The Good Book Company, 2022), 58.

4. Ortlund, *Marriage and the Mystery of the Gospel*, 11–14, 107–12.

5. The ESV reads "jealousy," which is not wrong. But "passion" better suits the parallelism. See Robert Gordis, *The Song of Songs and Lamentations: A Study, Modern Translation and Commentary*, revised edition (New York: KTAV Publishing House, 1974), 99.

6. Dietrich Bonhoeffer, *Letters and Papers from Prison* (London: SCM Press, 1967), 49.

Chapter 4

1. Walter Hooper, ed., *The Collected Letters of C. S. Lewis* (New York: HarperCollins, 2007), III:608.

2. https://godrules.net/library/spurgeon/45spurgeon4.htm

3. Edith Schaeffer, *What Is a Family?* (Old Tappan: Revell, 1975), 47. Italics original.

4. "Claim Your Children for Christ," a sermon preached at Lake Avenue Congregational Church, Pasadena, California, May 16, 1976.

Chapter 5

1. John S. C. Abbott, *The Mother at Home* (Boston: Crocker & Brewster, 1835), 159.

2. Jochem Douma, *The Ten Commandments: Manual for the Christian Life* (Phillipsburg, NJ: P&R Publishing, 1996), 172.

3. This story is told in Jani Ortlund, *Fearlessly Feminine, Boldly Living God's Plan for Womanhood* (Sisters, OR: Multnomah, 2000), 129.

4. https://www.youtube.com/watch?v=5VkNNeMgZcY, accessed May 25, 2023.

5. J. C. Ryle, *The Duties of Parents* (Warrendale, PA: Ichthus Publications, 2014), 14.

6. Andrew Peterson, *The God of the Garden: Thoughts on Creation, Culture, and the Kingdom* (Nashville: B&H, 2021), 118.

7. Václav Havel, *Open Letters: Selected Writings, 1965–1990* (New York: Alfred A. Knopf, 1991), 206:

> "Technology—that child of modern science, which in turn is a child of modern metaphysics—is out of humanity's control, has ceased to serve us, has enslaved us and compelled us to participate in the preparation of our own destruction. . . . We look on helplessly as that coldly functioning machine we have created inevitably engulfs us, tearing us away from our natural affiliations."

8. T. S. Eliot, "Preface," in Simone Weil, *The Need for Roots: Prelude to a Declaration of Duties towards Mankind* (London: Routledge, Taylor & Francis Group, 1952), xiv.

Chapter 6

1. Raymond C. Ortlund, *Lord, Make My Life a Miracle!* (Ventura: Regal Books, 1974), 60.

2. Simone Weil, *The Need for Roots: Prelude to a Declaration of Duties towards Mankind* (London: Routledge, Taylor & Francis Group, 1952), 43.

3. Os Guinness, *A Free People's Suicide: Sustainable Freedom and the American Future* (Downers Grove, IL: InterVarsity Press, 2012), 83.

4. Patrick Fairbairn, in *The Revival of Religion: Addresses by Scottish Evangelical Leaders Delivered in Glasgow in 1840* (Edinburgh: The Banner of Truth Trust, 1984), 373–74.

Chapter 7

1. We are not disparaging these lesser matters. We just agree with C. S. Lewis: "Put first things first and we get second things thrown in; put second things first and we lose *both* first and second things." Walter Hooper, ed., *The Collected Letters of C. S. Lewis, Volume III* (San Francisco: HarperCollins, 2007), 111. Lewis put it yet another way: "You can't get second things by putting them first; you can get second things only by putting first things first." C. S. Lewis, *God in the Dock: Essays on Theology and Ethics* (Grand Rapids: Eerdmans, 1970), 280.

2. J. I. Packer and Carolyn Nystrom, *Praying: Finding Our Way through Duty to Delight* (Downers Grove, IL: IVP Books, 2006), 175.

3. Paul Johnson, *A History of the Modern World: From 1917 to the 1980s* (London: Weidenfeld and Nicolson, 1983), 698.

4. "Claim Your Children for Christ," a sermon preached at Lake Avenue Congregational Church, Pasadena, California, May 16, 1976.

Chapter 8

1. J. I. Packer, *Concise Theology: A Guide to Historic Christian Beliefs* (Wheaton: Tyndale House, 1993), 162.

2. https://www.luther.de/en/95thesen.html

3. Jack Miller, quoted in Stephen Smallman, *The Walk: Steps for New and Renewed Followers of Jesus* (Phillipsburg, NJ: P&R Publishing, 2009), 106.

4. Walter Hooper, in C. S. Lewis, *God in the Dock: Essays on Theology and Ethics* (Grand Rapids: Eerdmans, 1973), 12.

5. John Stott, *Confess Your Sins: The Way of Reconciliation* (Grand Rapids: Eerdmans, 2017), 29.

6. Corrie ten Boom, *Tramp for The Lord* (Old Tappan, NJ: Fleming H. Revell, 1974), 55.

7. C. S. Lewis, *The Lion, The Witch and The Wardrobe: A Story for Children* (New York: Collier Books, 1972), 136.

8. For the form or outline of this prayer, see https://timothy keller.com/blog/2010/10/1/how-to-pray-better-in-public-and-in -private-too, accessed May 20, 2023.

Chapter 9

1. Matthew Henry, *Commentary on the Whole Bible* (McLean: MacDonald Publishing Company, 1985 reprint), V:589.

2. C. S. Lewis, *The Screwtape Letters* (New York: Simon & Schuster, 1996), 42.

3. Charles Bridges, *A Commentary on Proverbs* (Edinburgh: The Banner of Truth Trust, 1968), 3–4.

4. J. I. Packer, *Knowing God* (Downers Grove, IL: InterVarsity Press, 1973), "God Unchanging," 67–72.

5. Francis I. Anderson, "Yahweh, the Kind and Sensitive God," in Peter T. O'Brien and David G. Peterson, editors, *God Who Is Rich in Mercy: Essays Presented to Dr. D. B. Knox* (Grand Rapids: Baker Book House, 1986), 41–88.

6. Martin Luther, *A Commentary on St. Paul's Epistle to the Galatians* (London: James Clarke & Co., 1953), 40.

7. Taken from *The Book of Common Prayer* (Huntington Beach: Anglican Liturgy Press, 2019), 673.

Finally

1. Bruce K. Waltke, *An Old Testament Theology* (Grand Rapids: Zondervan, 2007), 287: "*Covenant* means 'a solemn commitment of oneself to undertake an obligation.'"

2. C. S. Lewis, ed., *Essays Presented to Charles Williams* (Grand Rapids: Eerdmans, 1974), 91.

Also available from Ray and Jani Ortlund

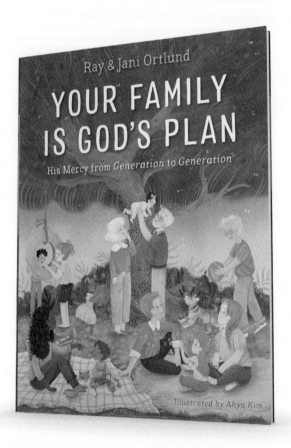

This unique picture book celebrates God's gift of families—from biblical times until today—and shows that families have always been a special part of God's plan!